Mandala
Luxurious Coloring

Copyright: Published in the United States by Janice Perrine
Published January 2017
ISBN-13: 978-1542642620
ISBN-10: 1542642620

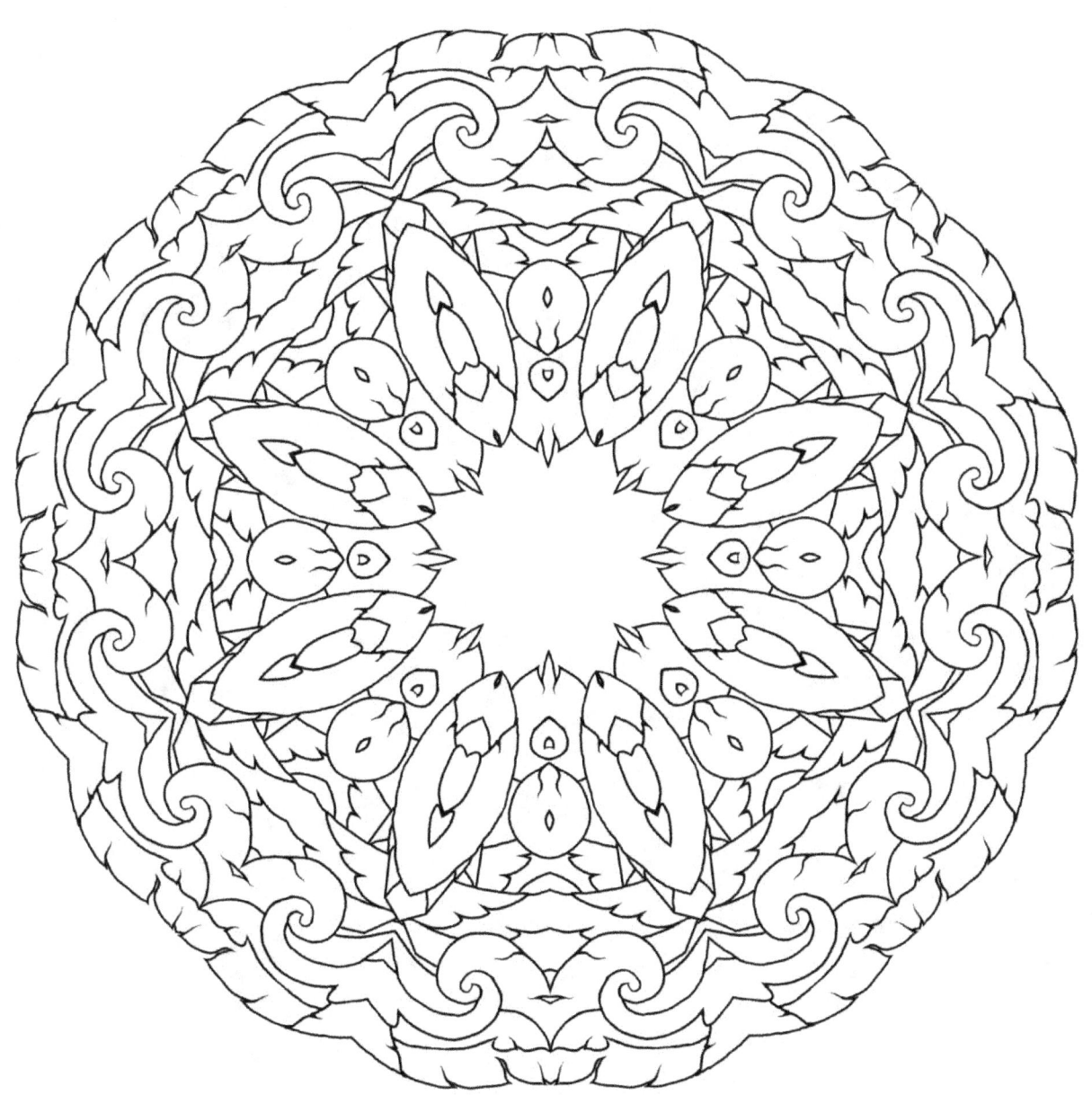

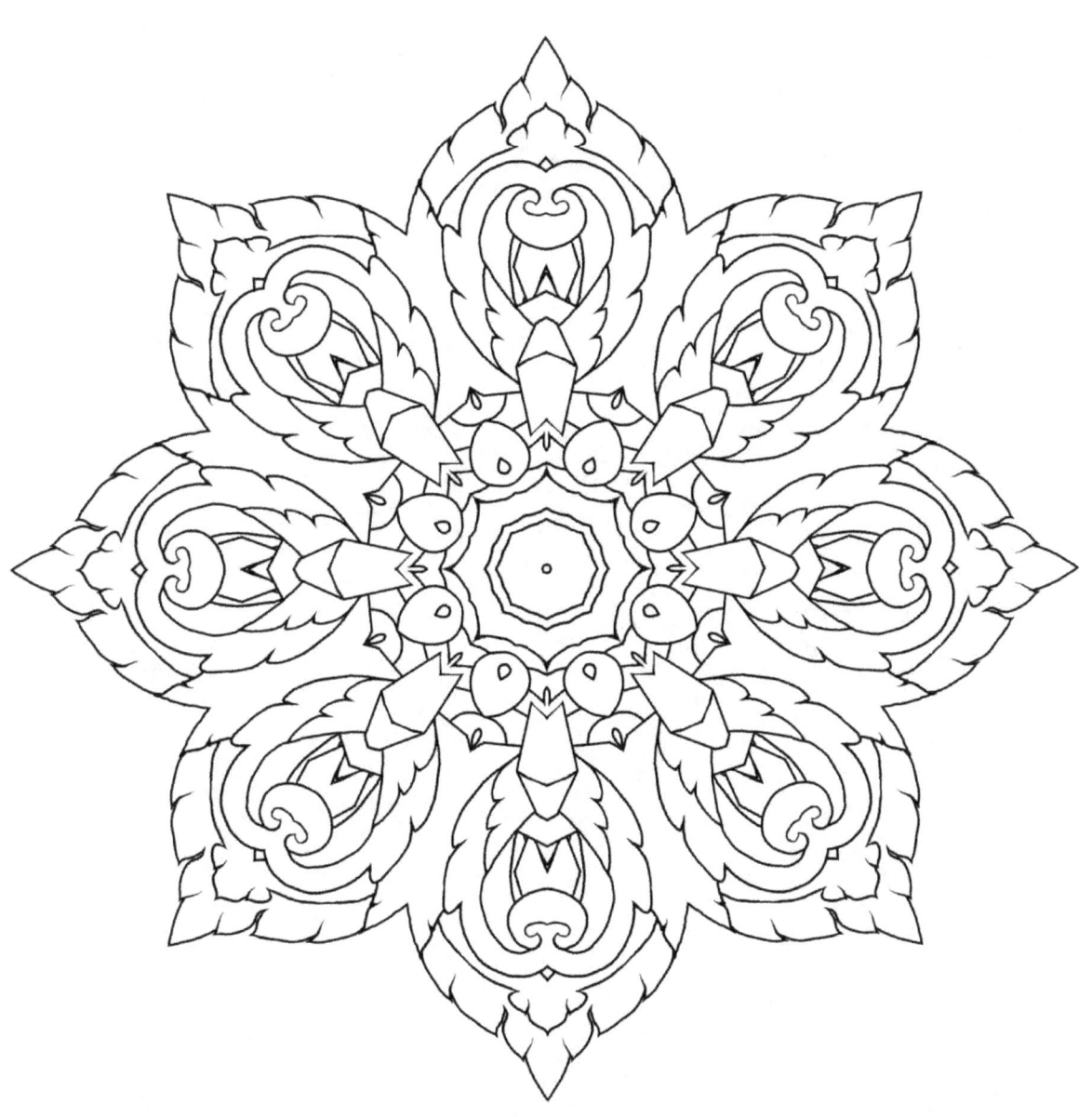

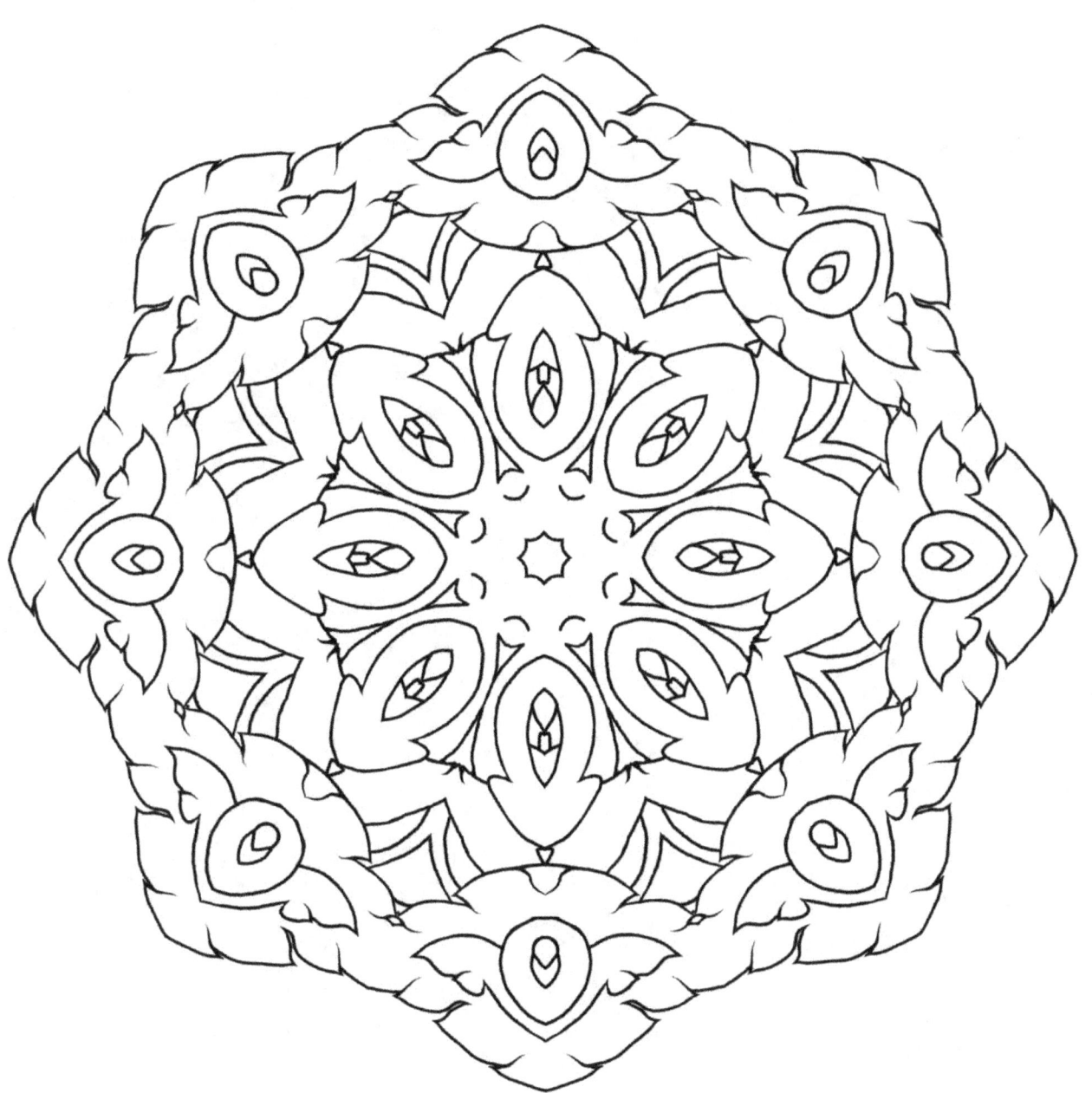

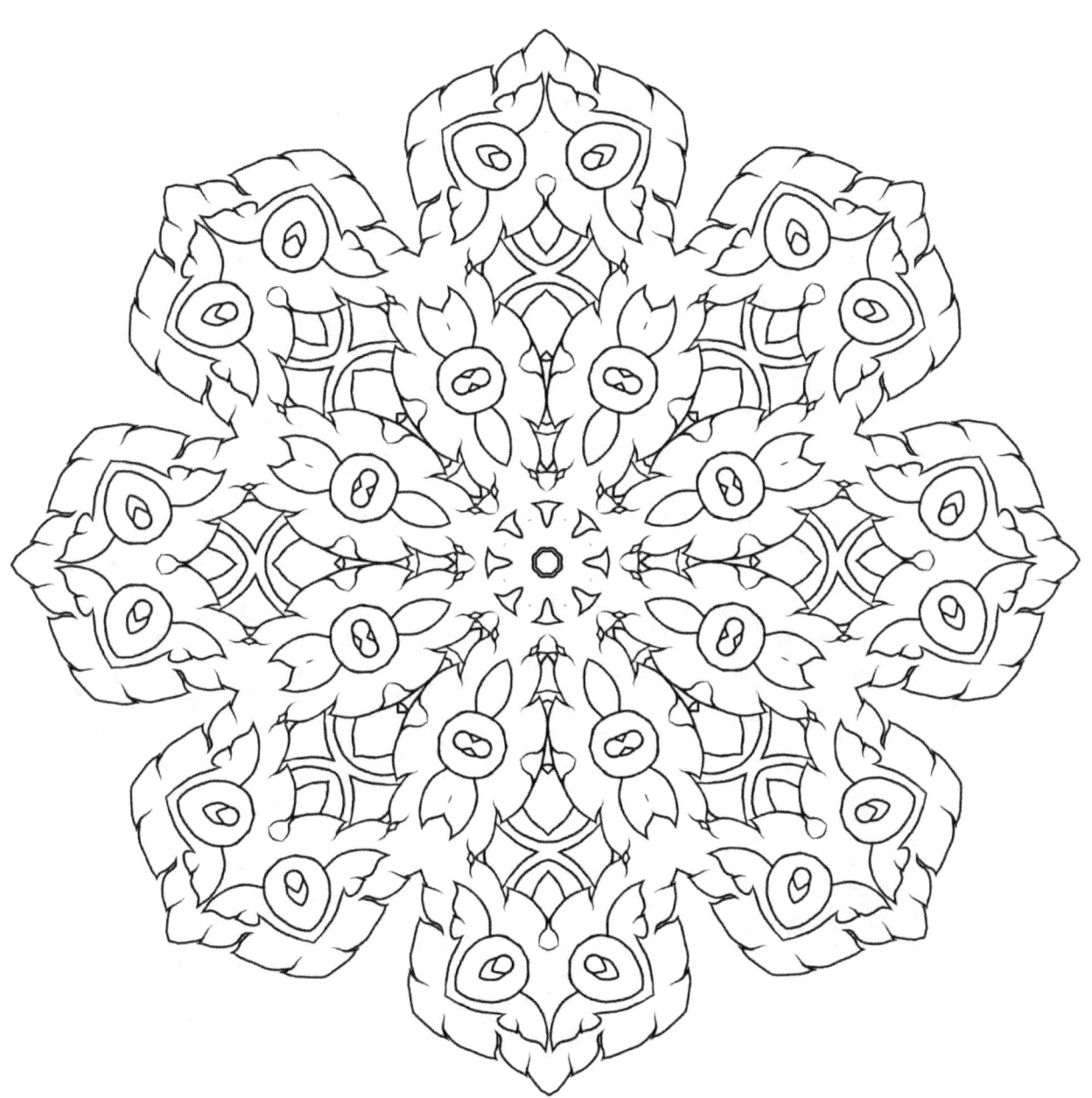

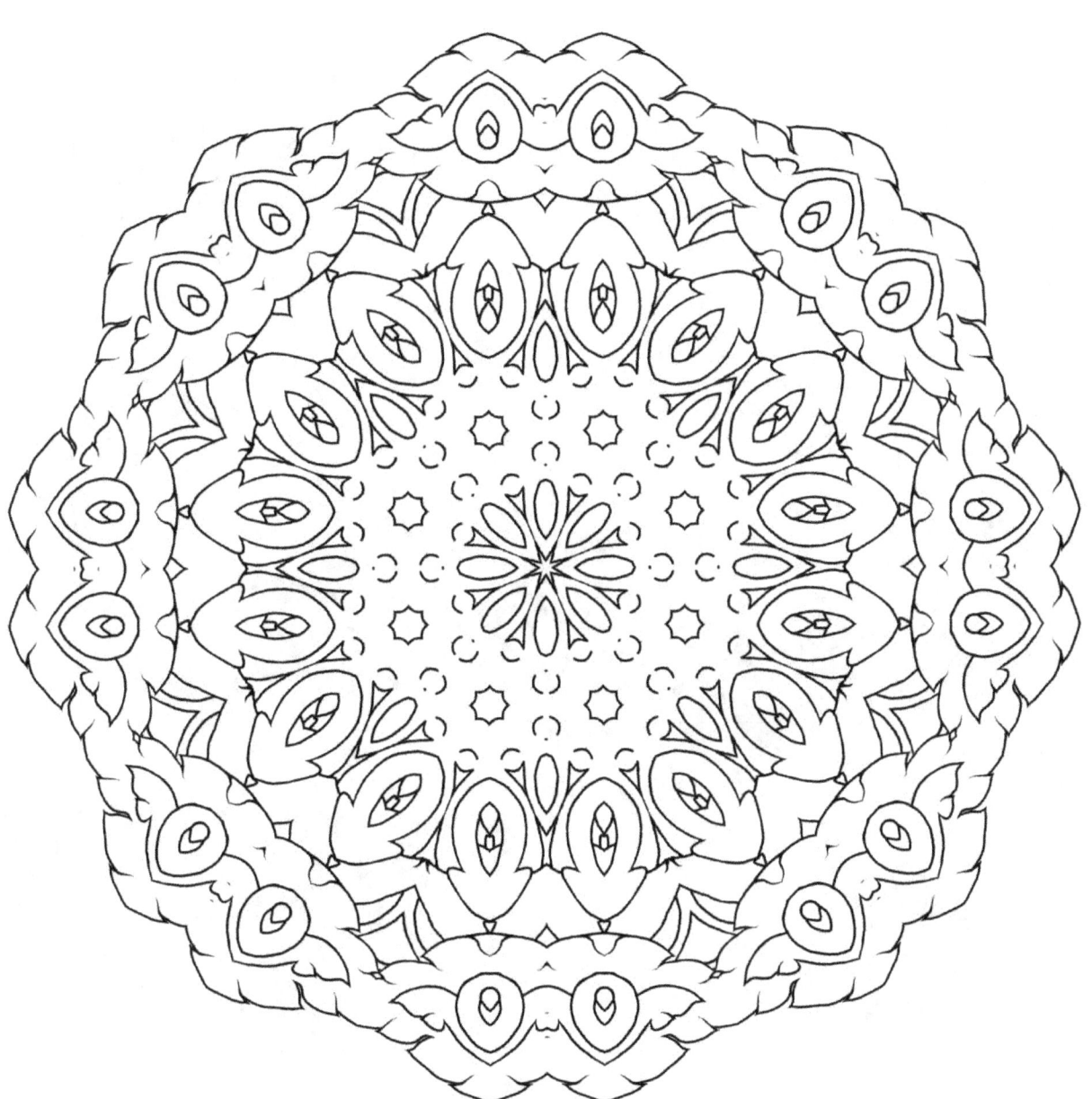

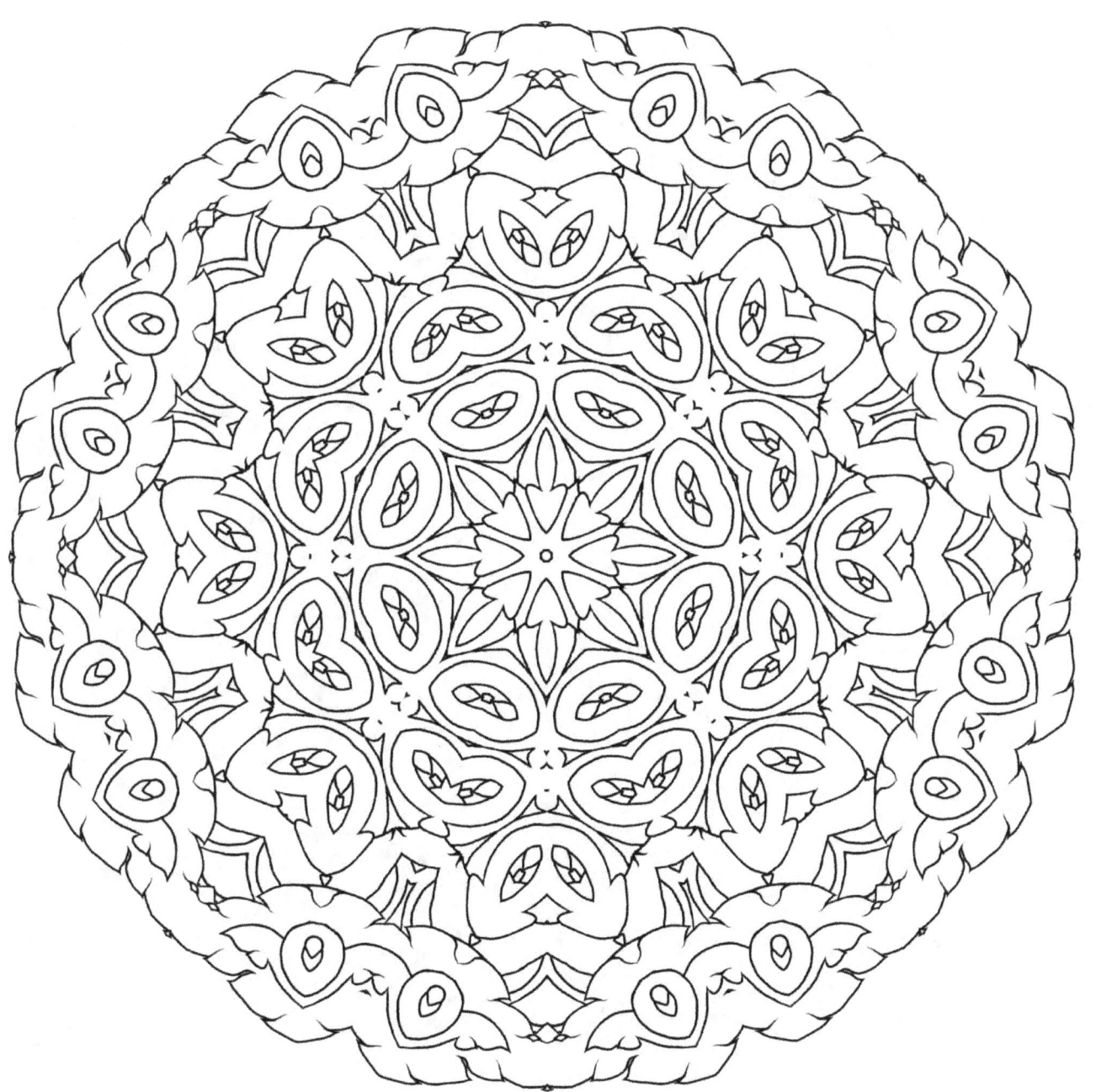

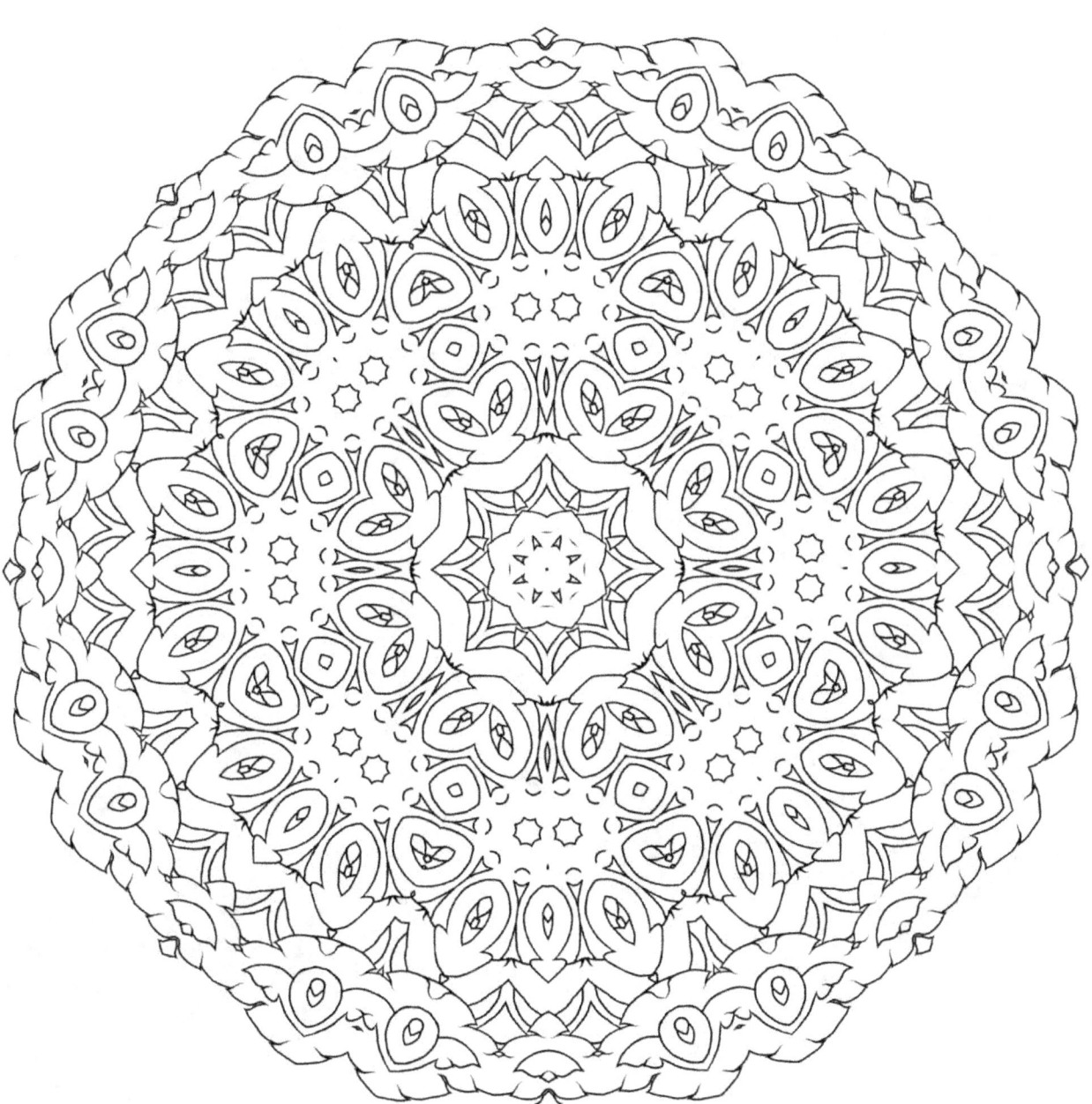

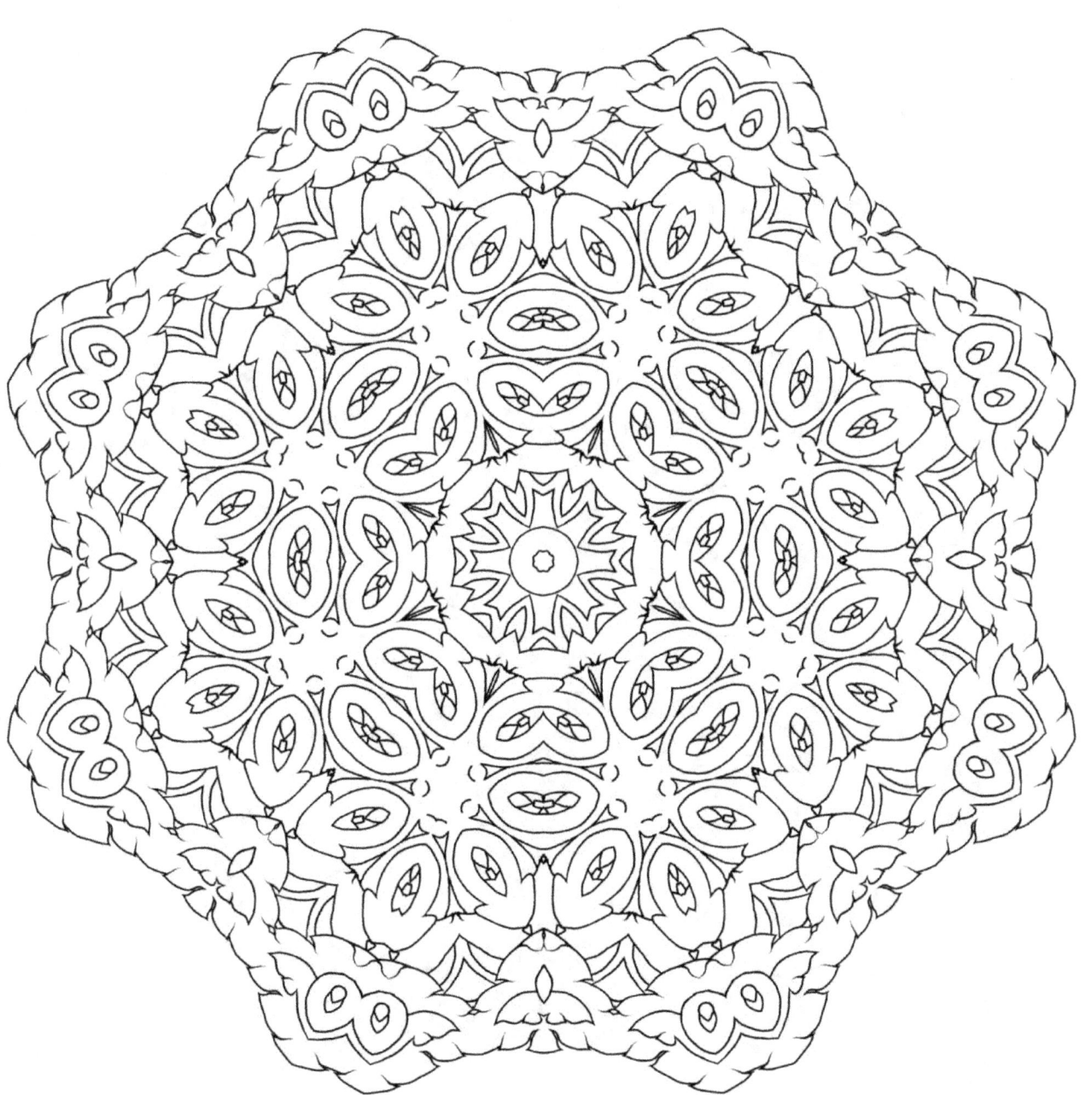

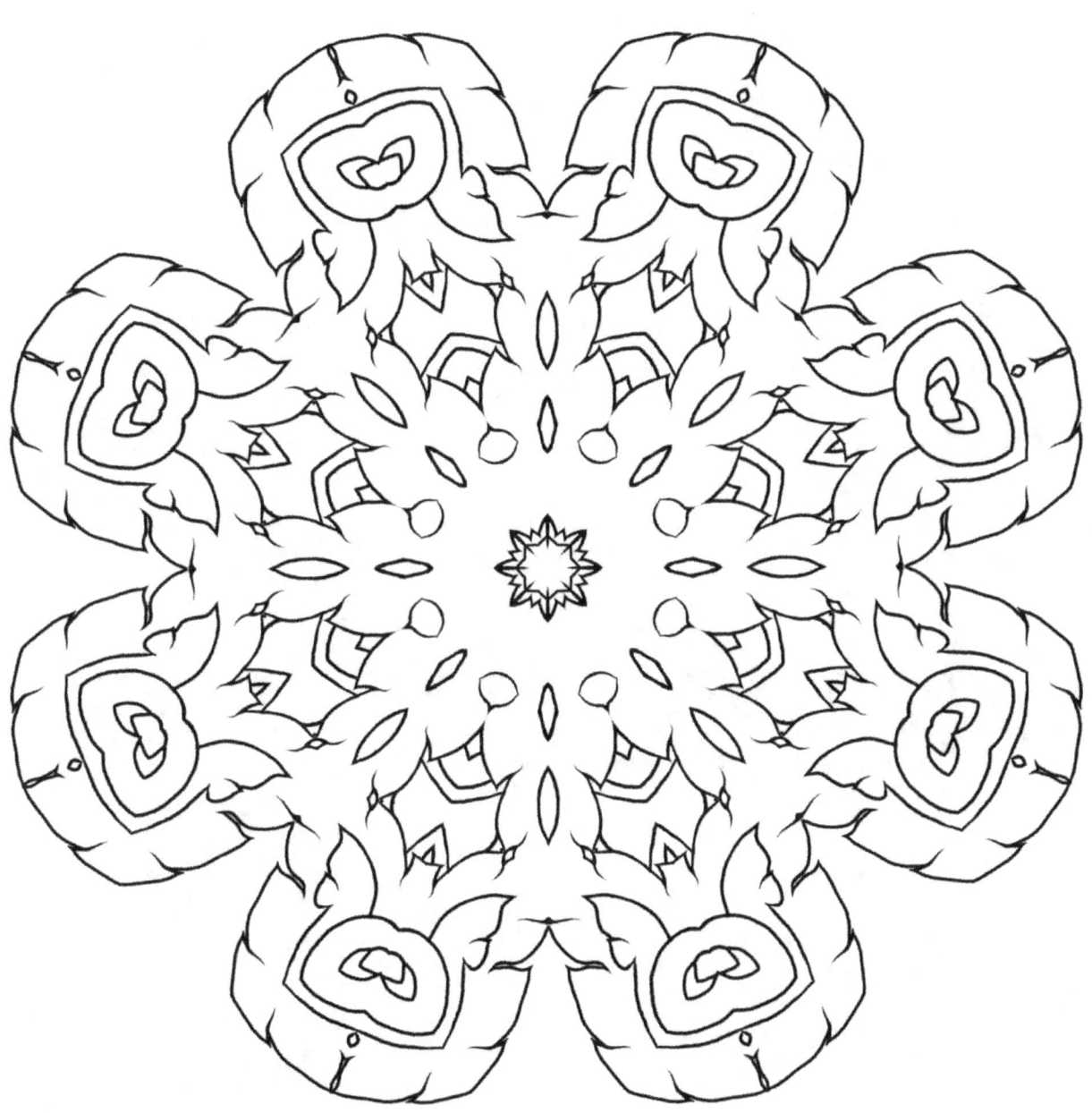

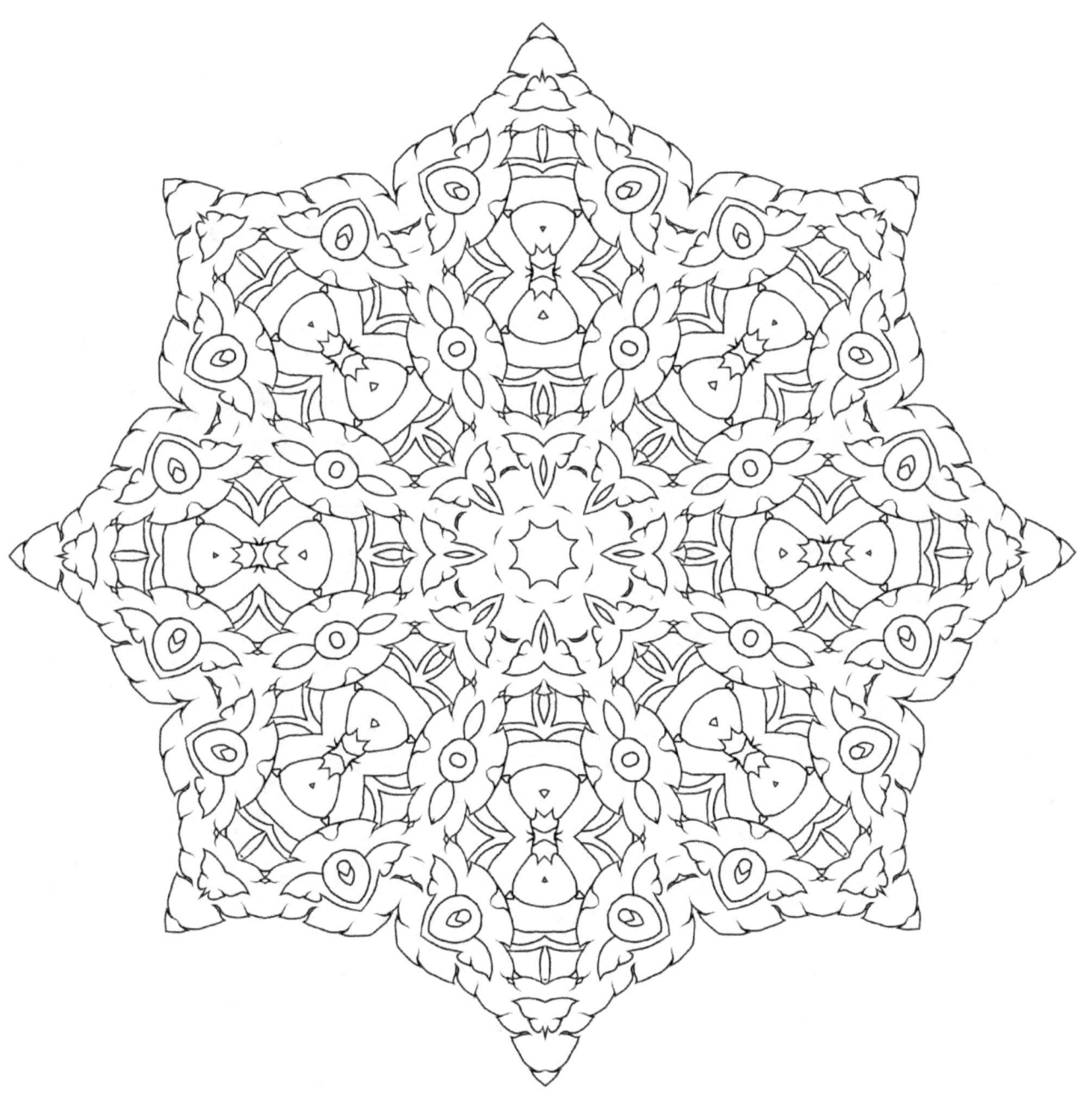

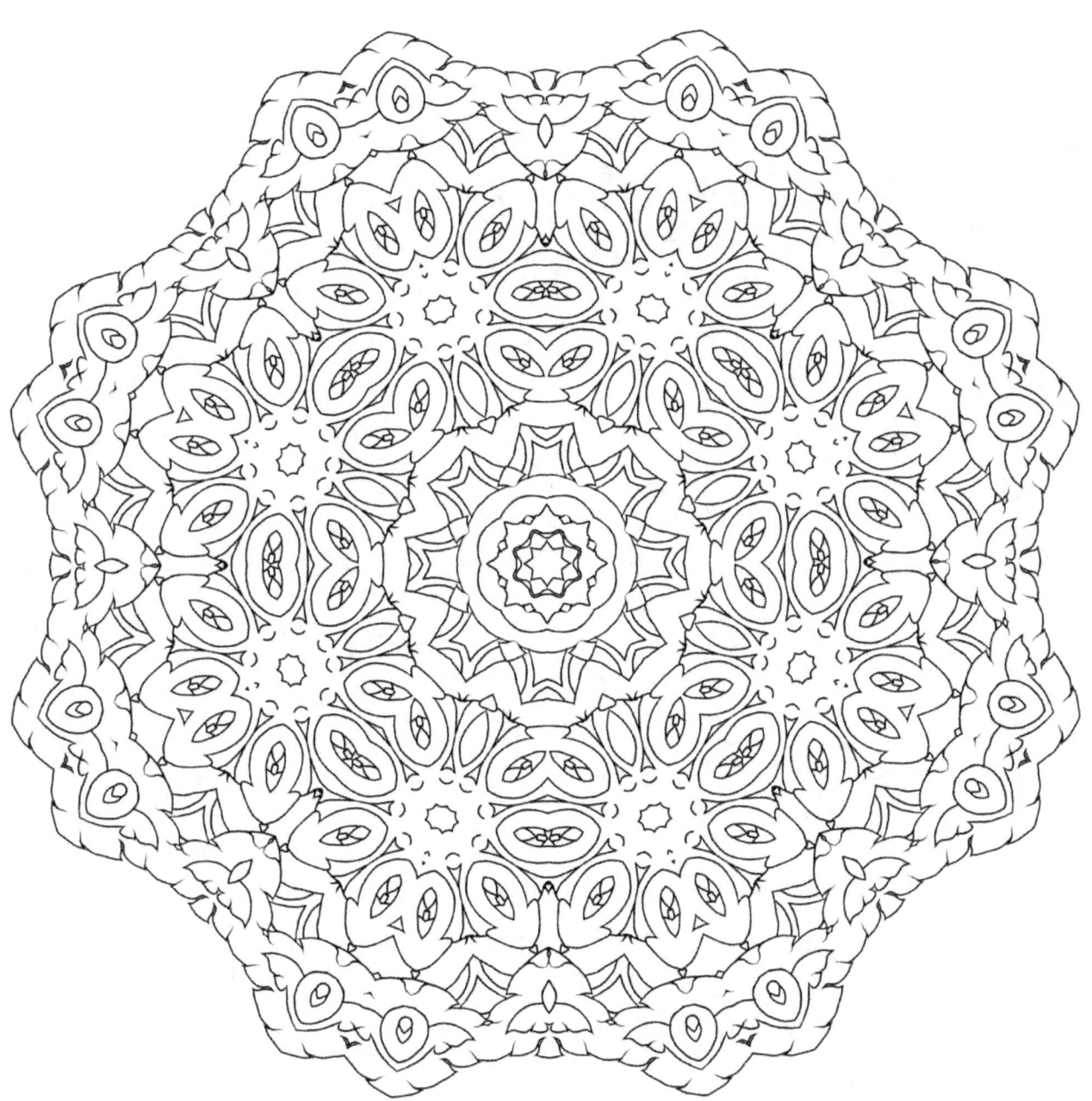

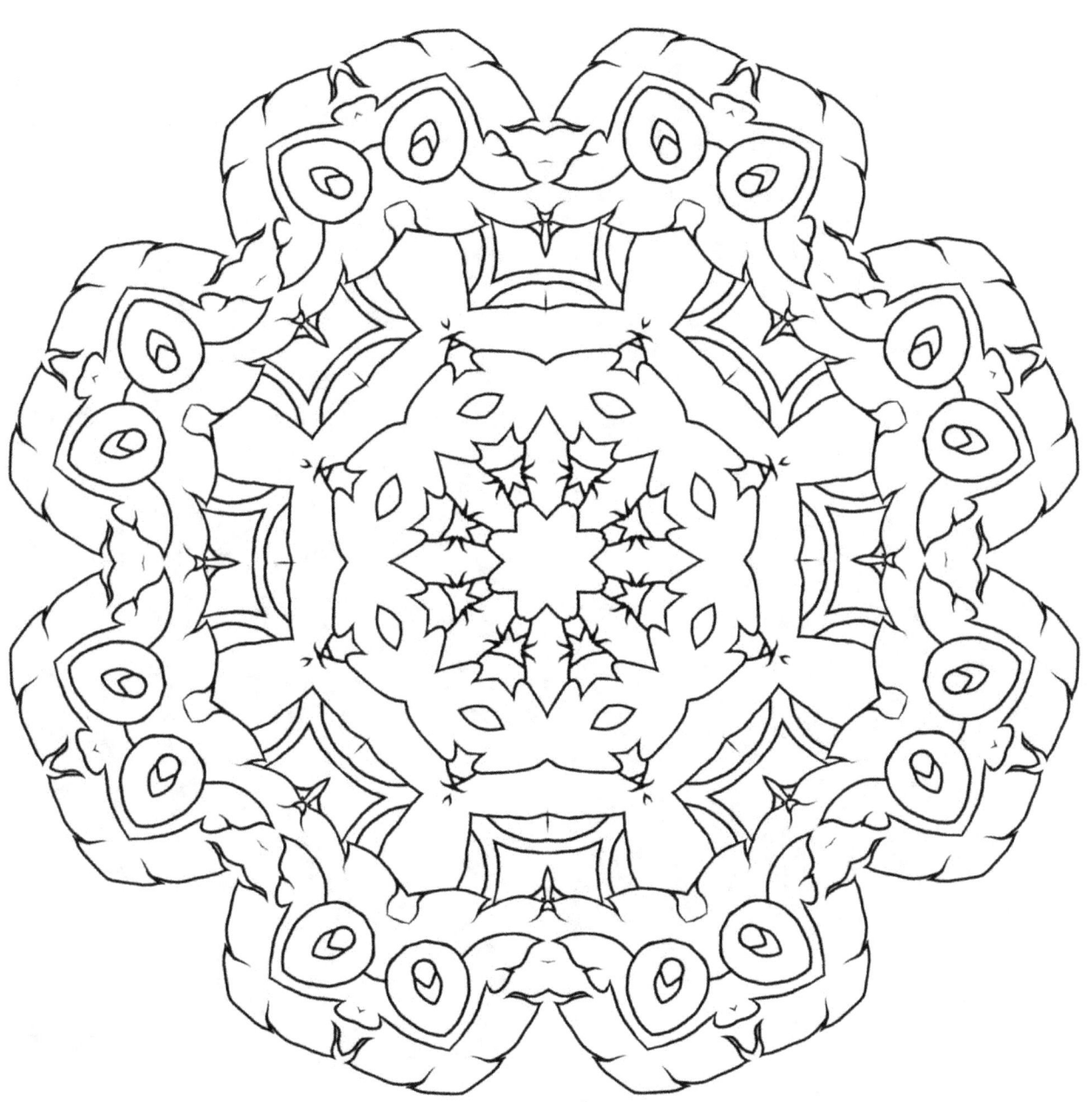

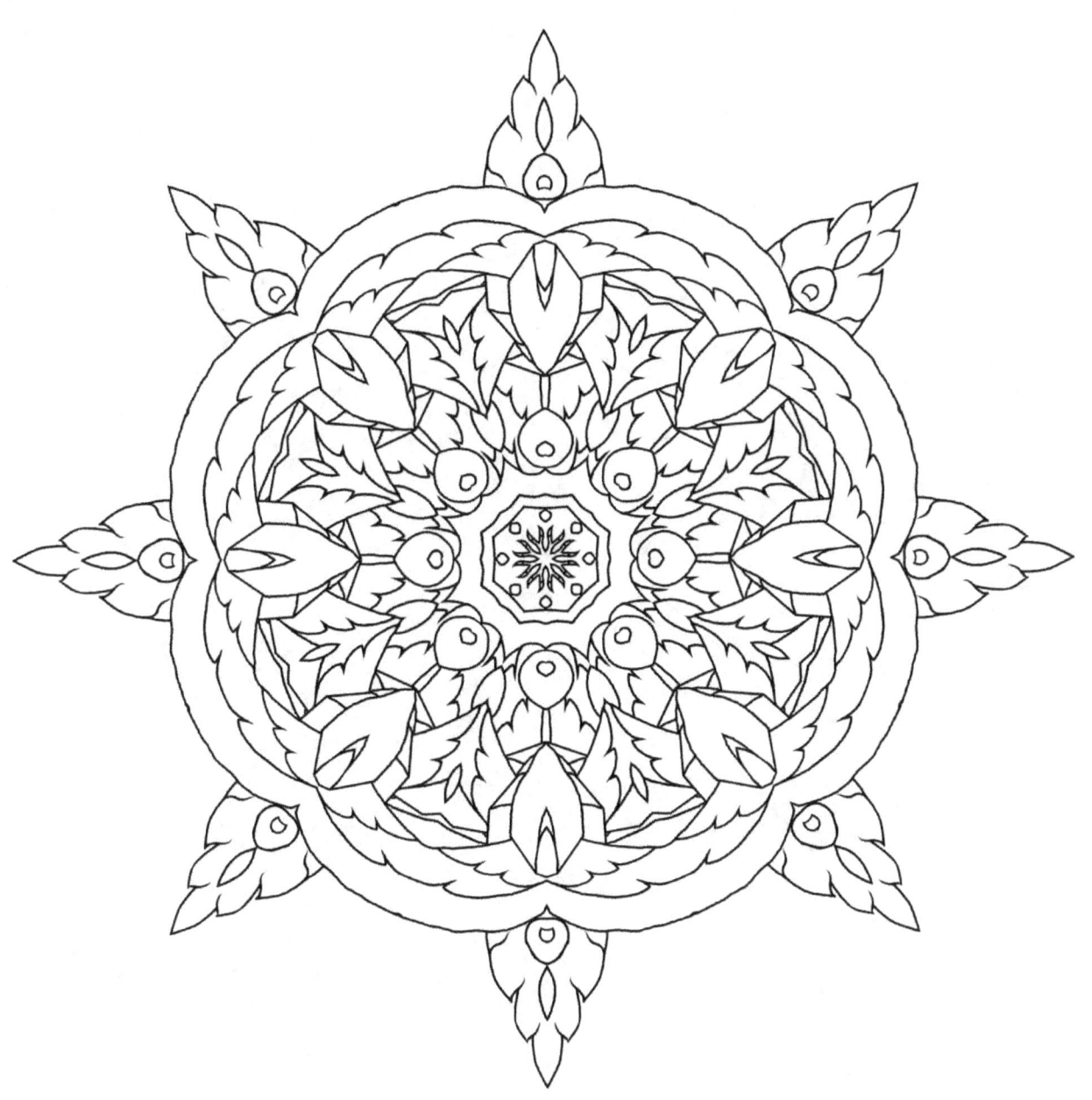

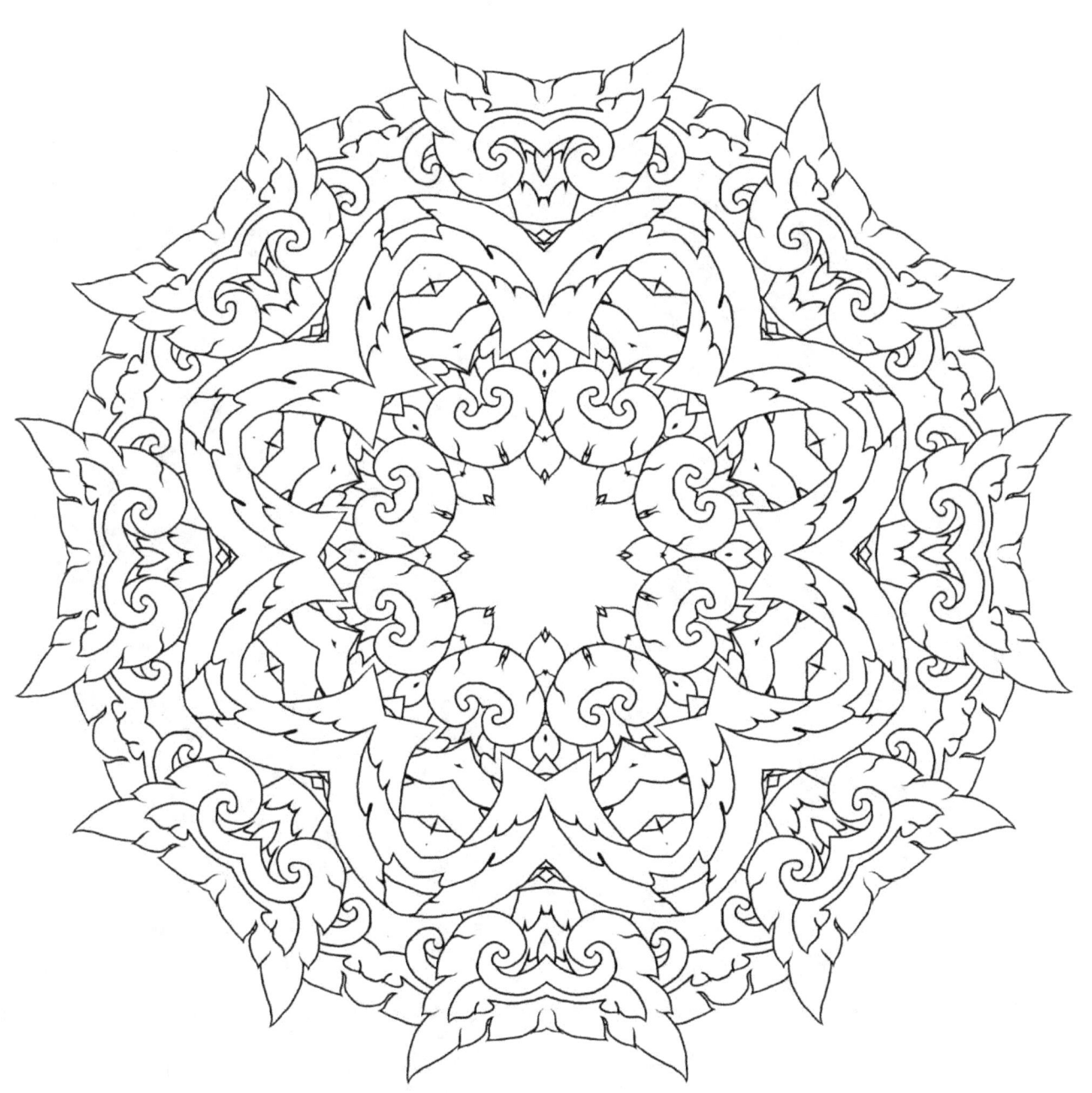

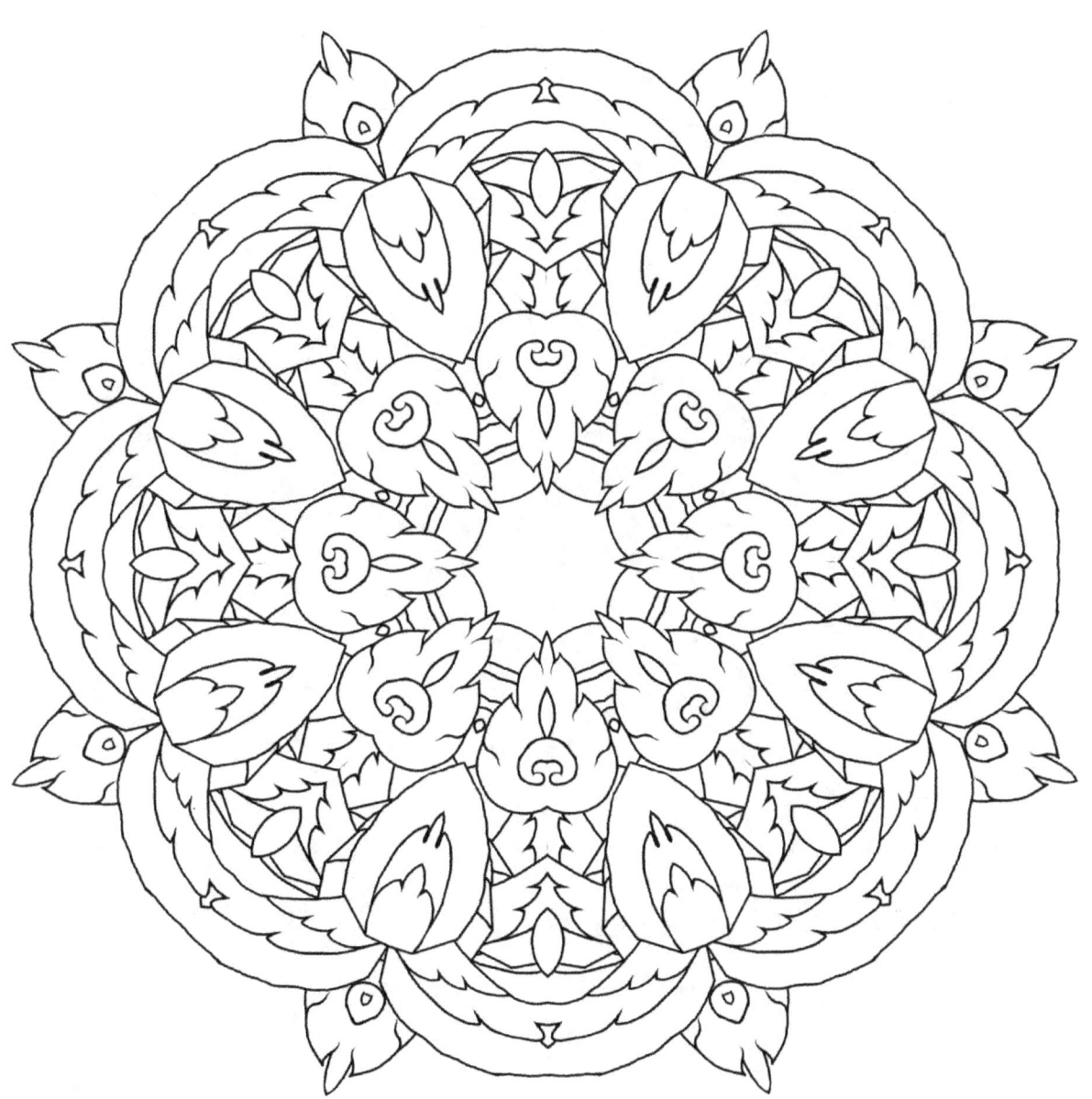

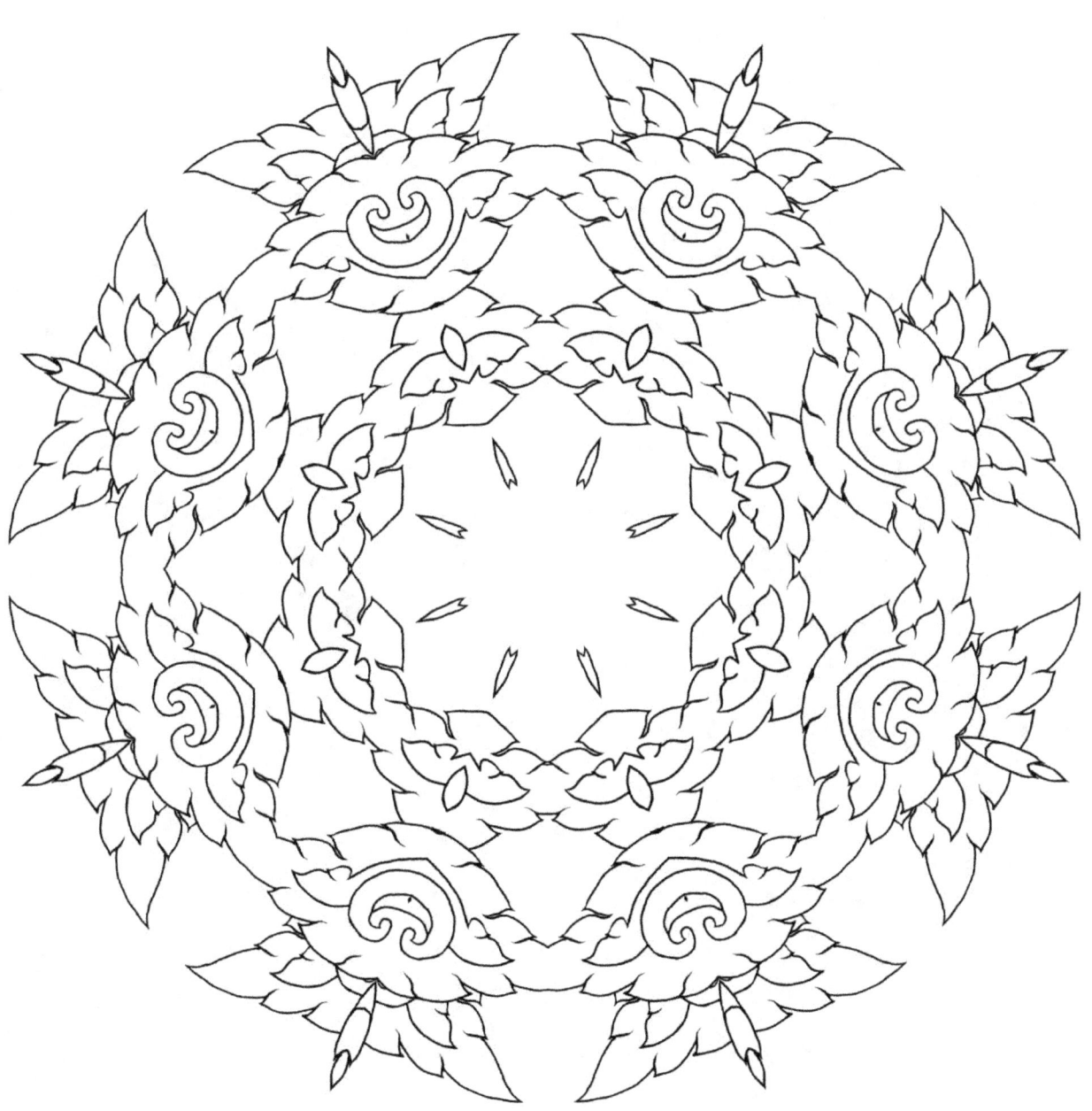

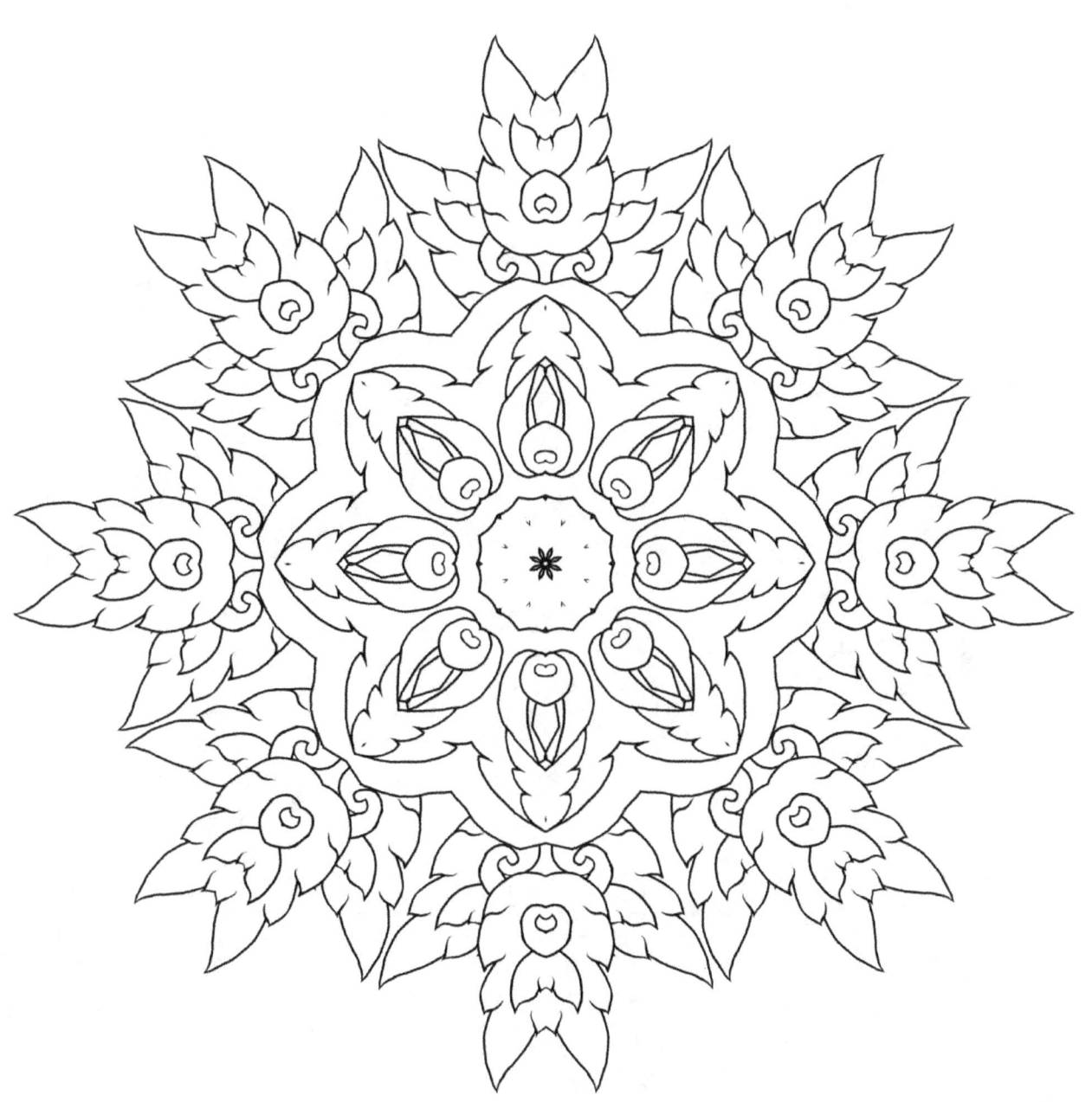

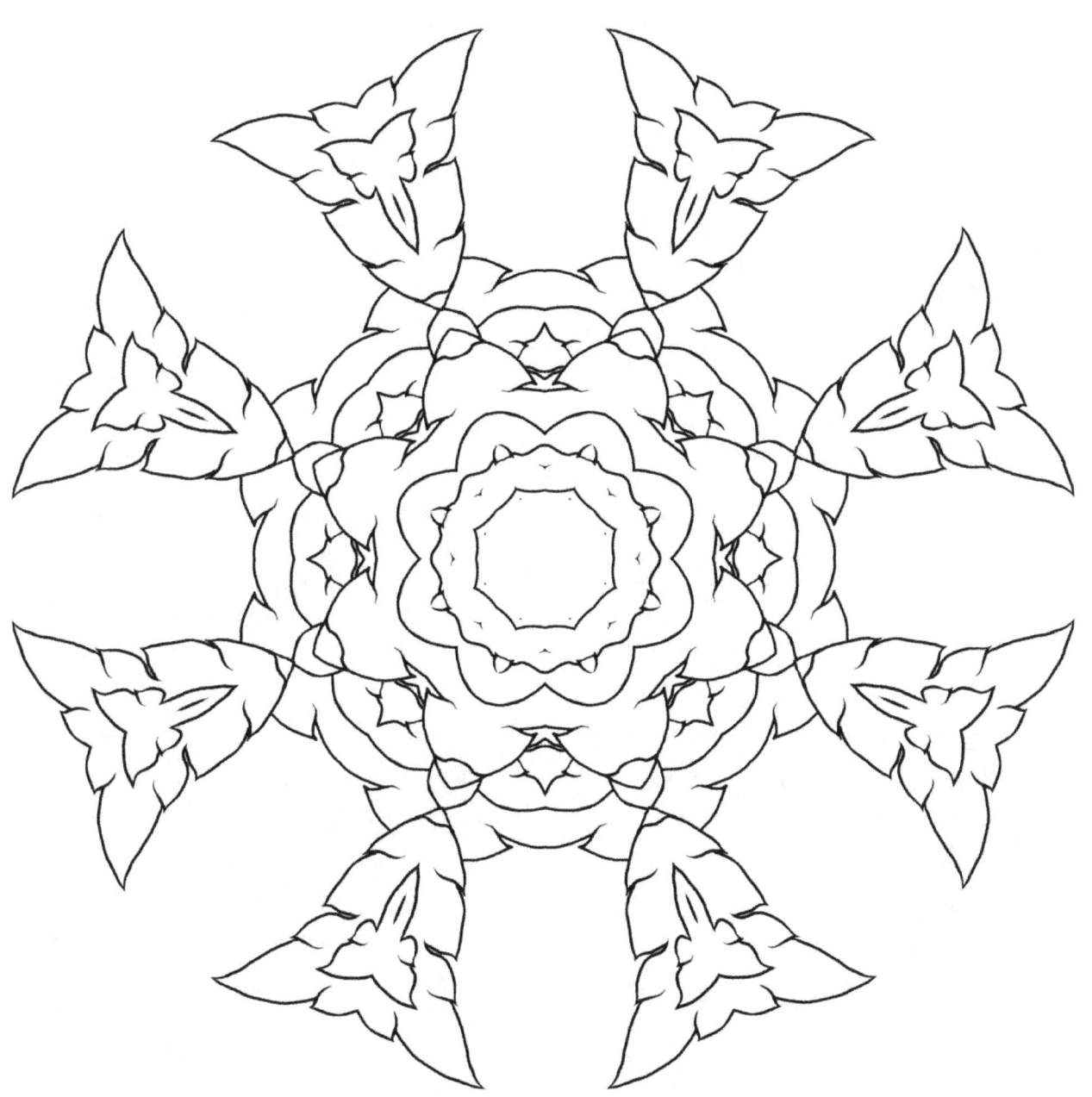

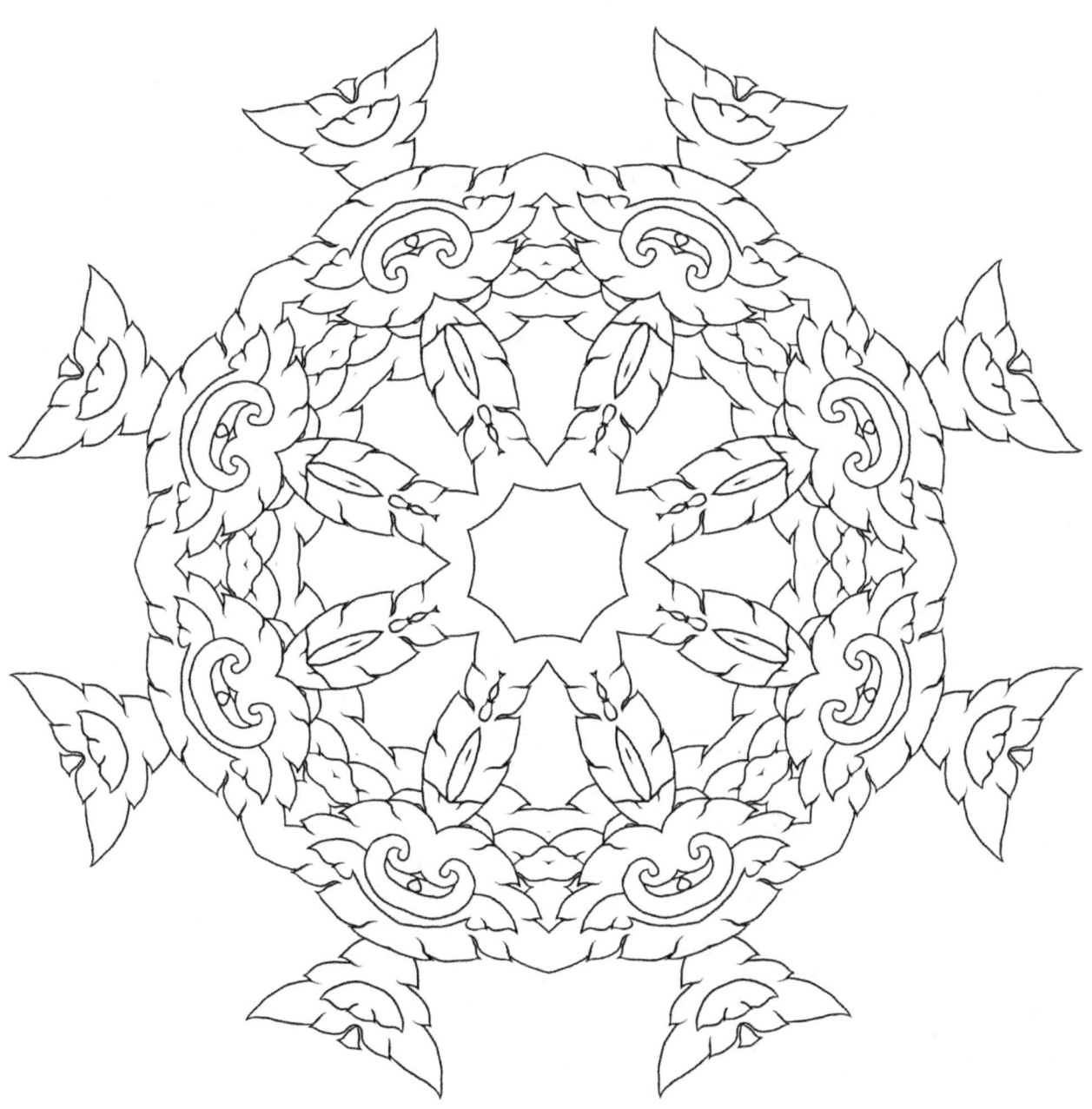

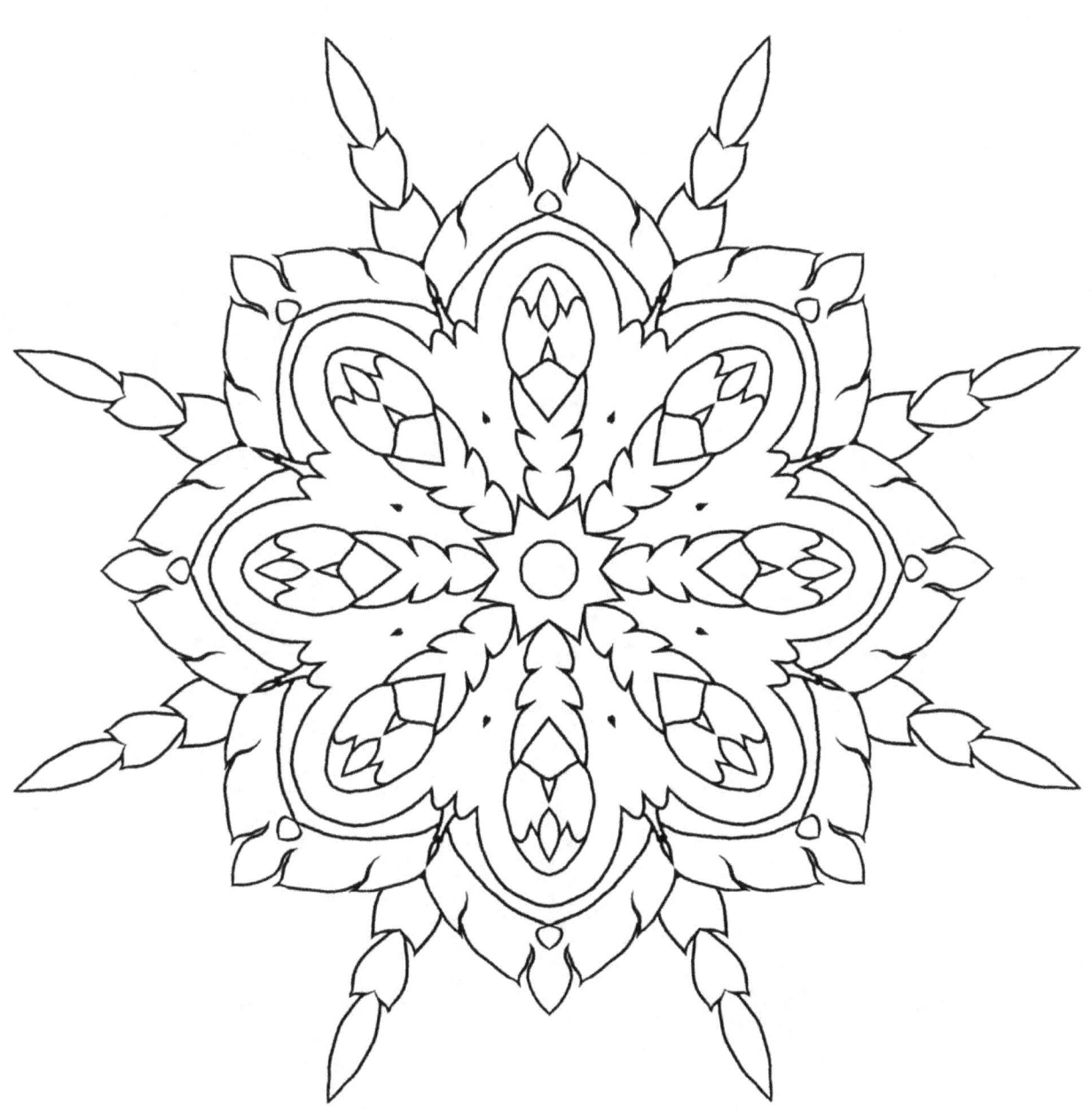

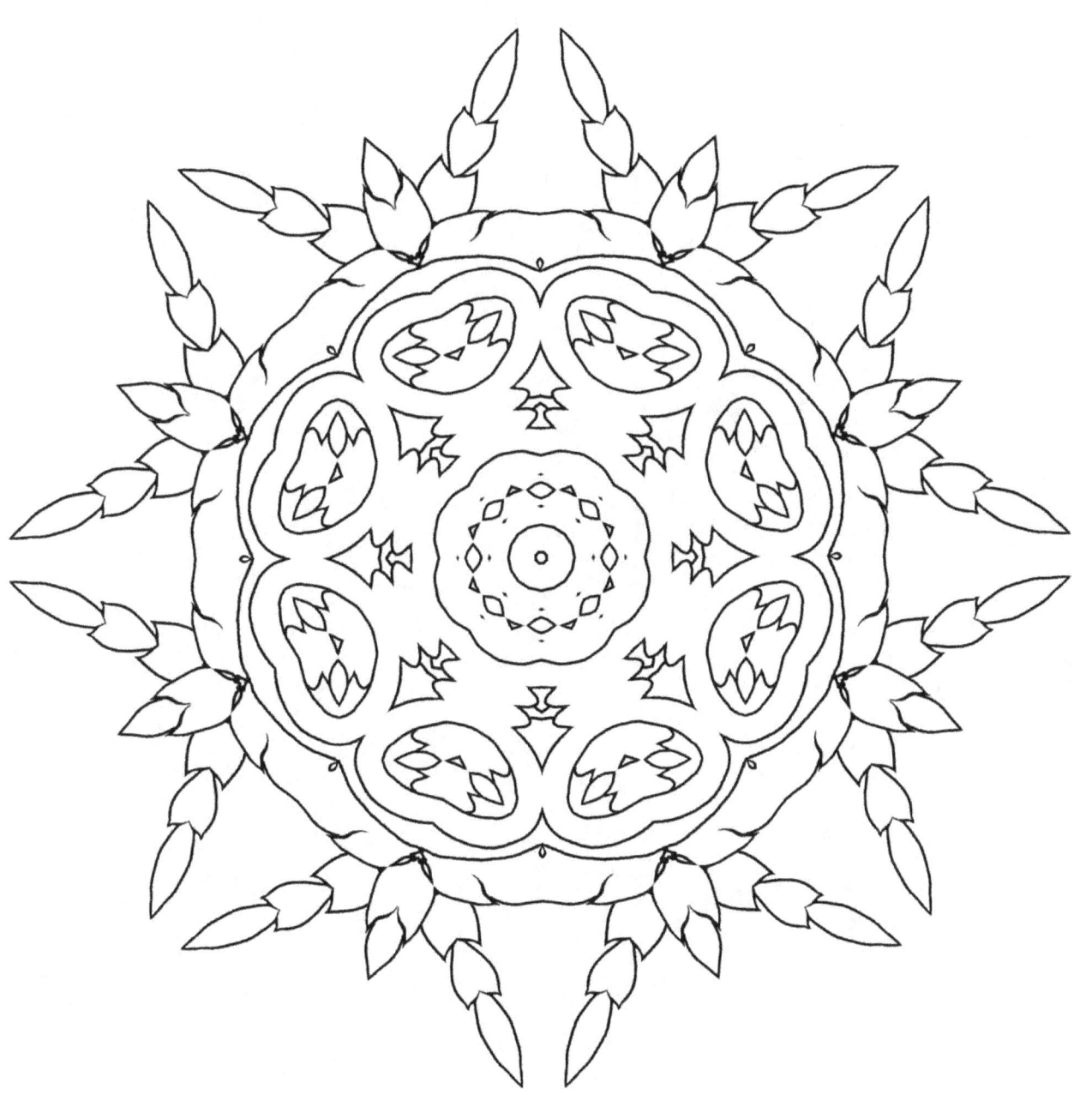

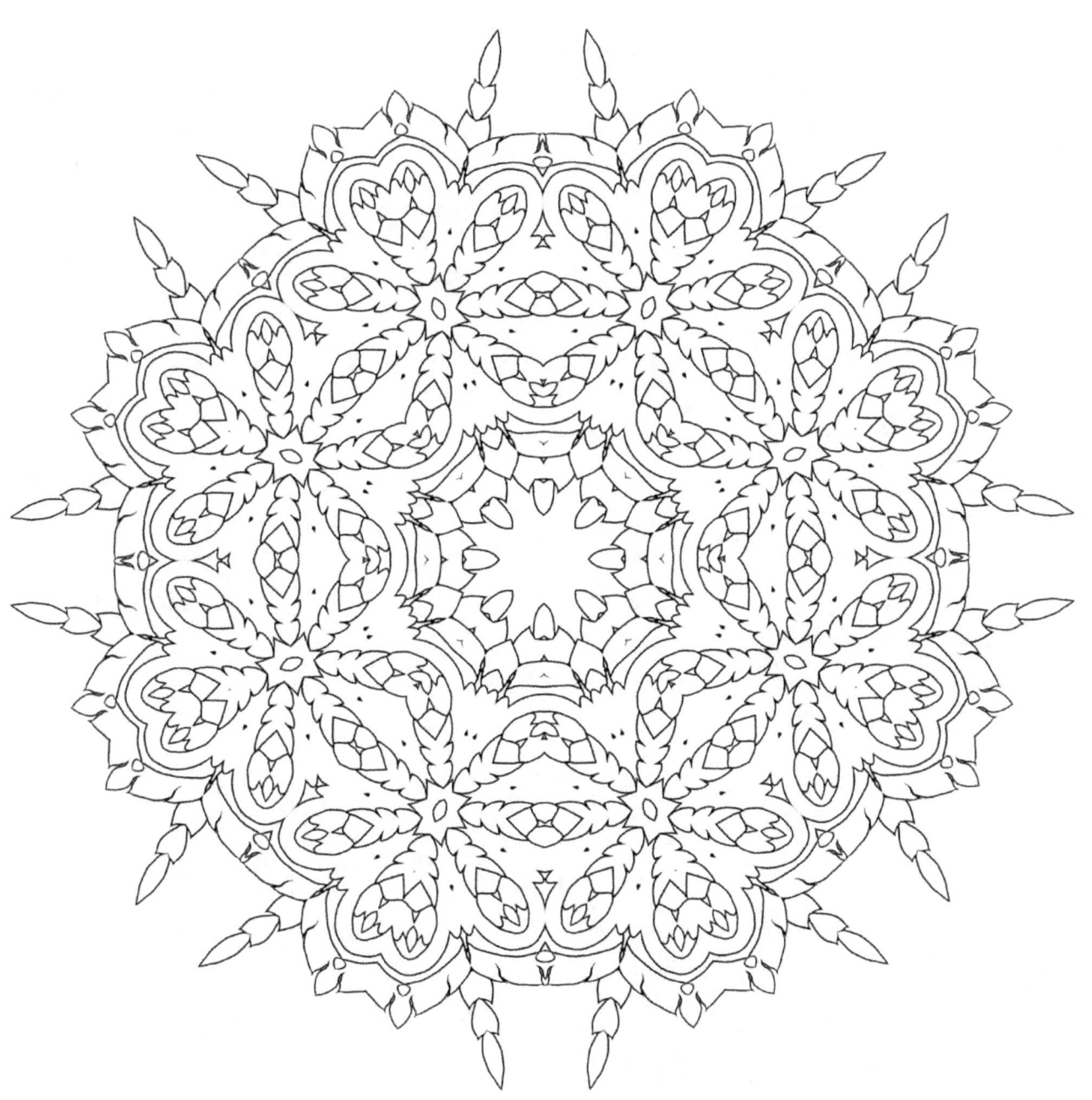

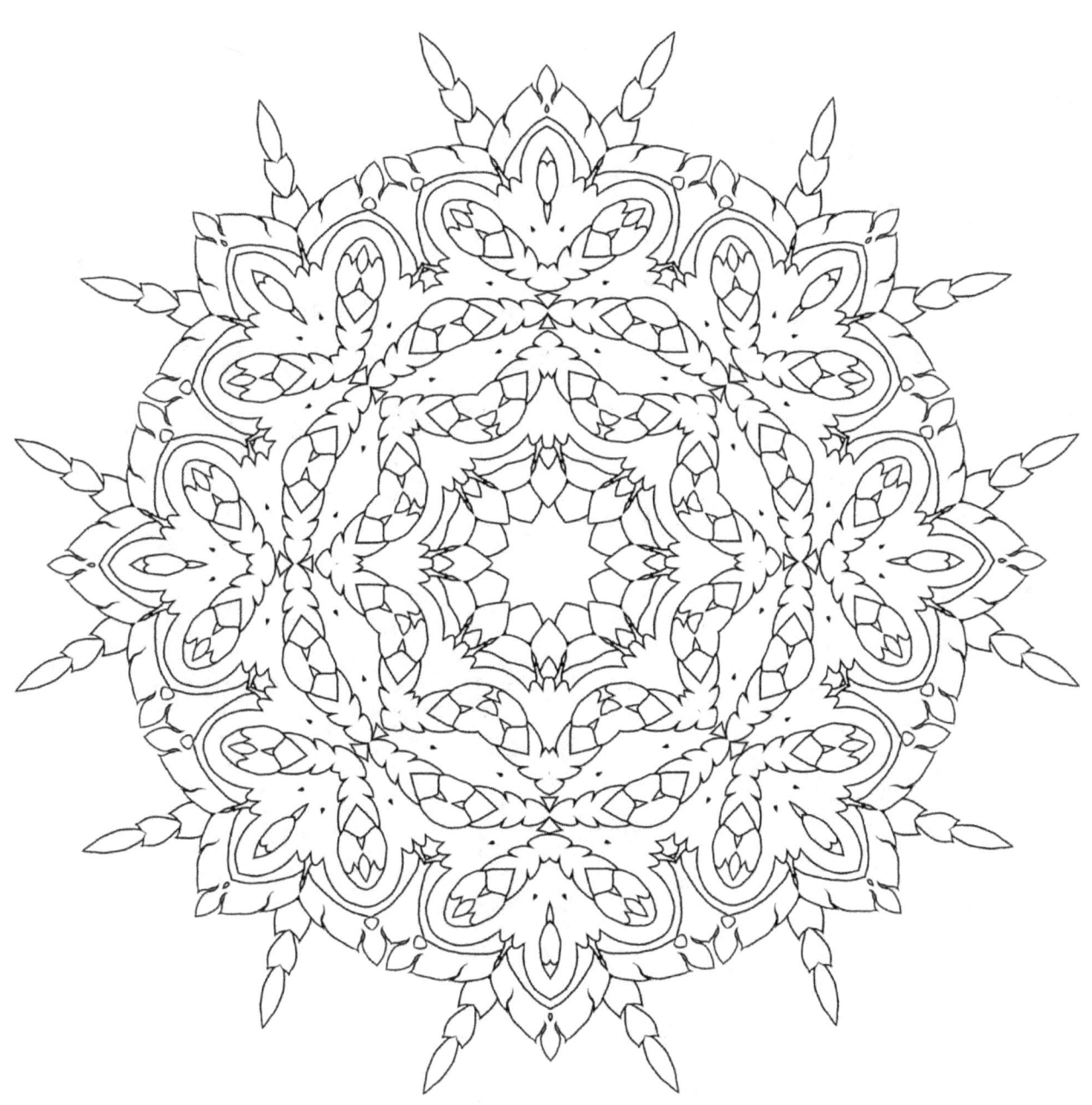

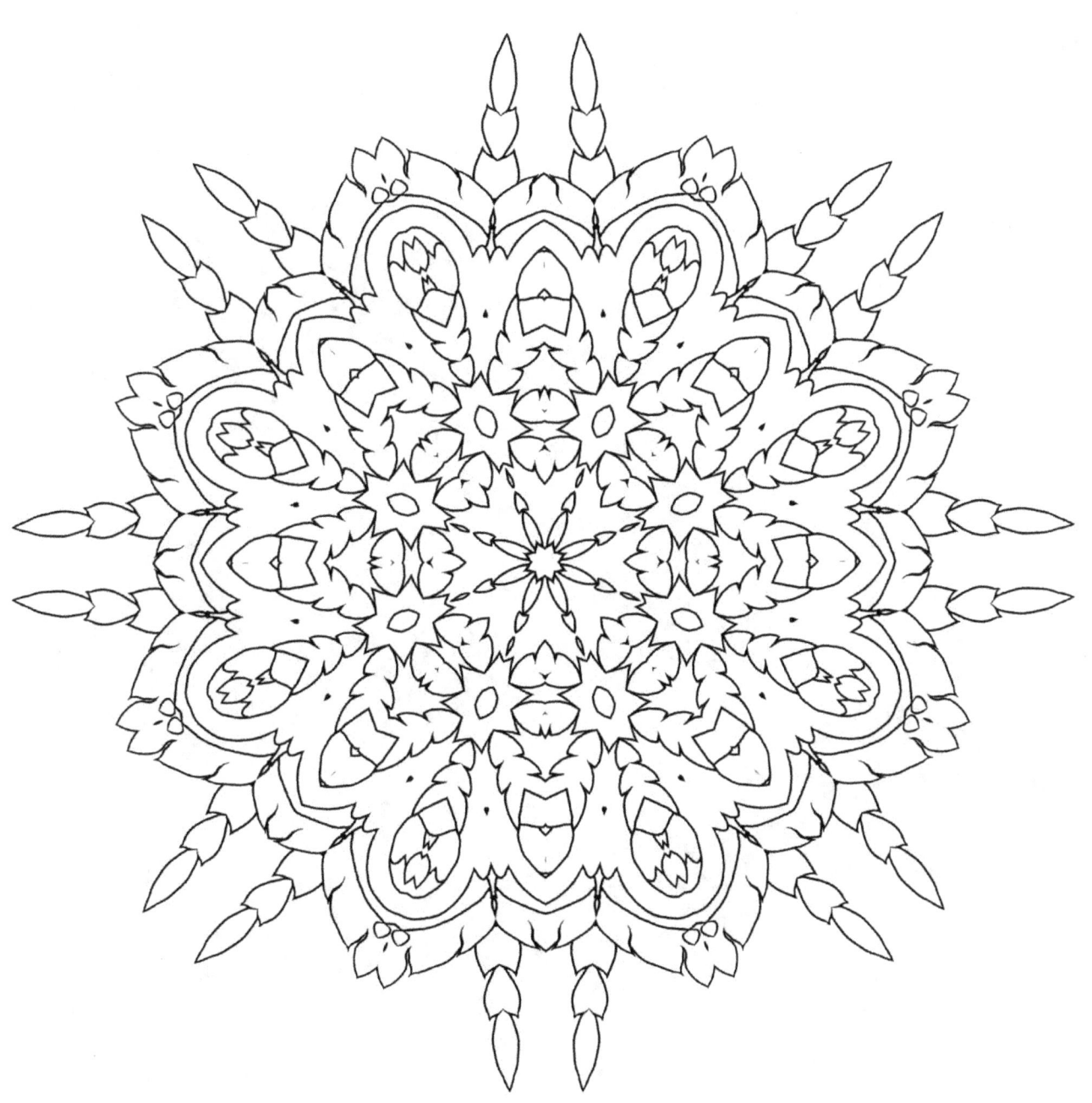

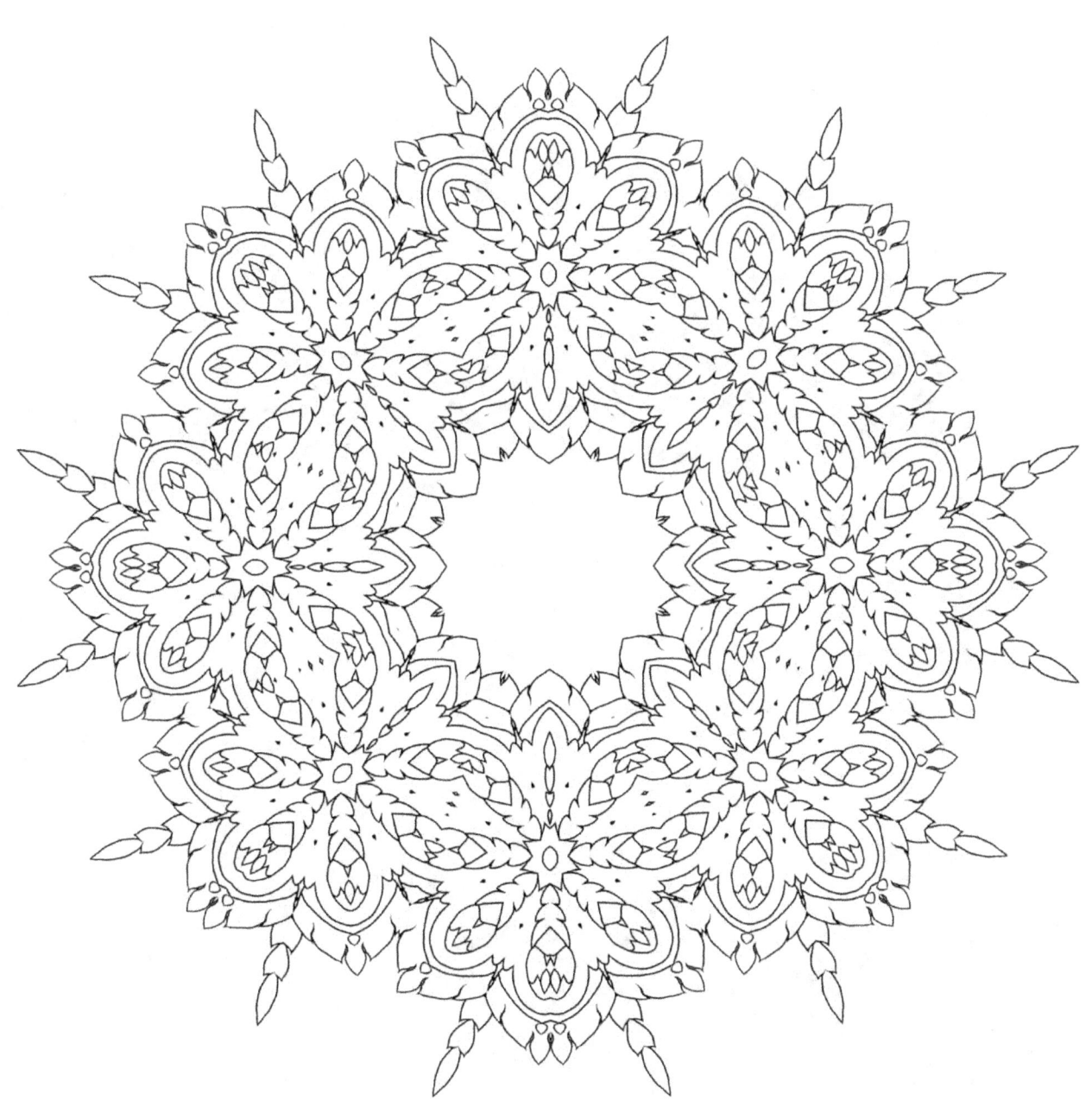

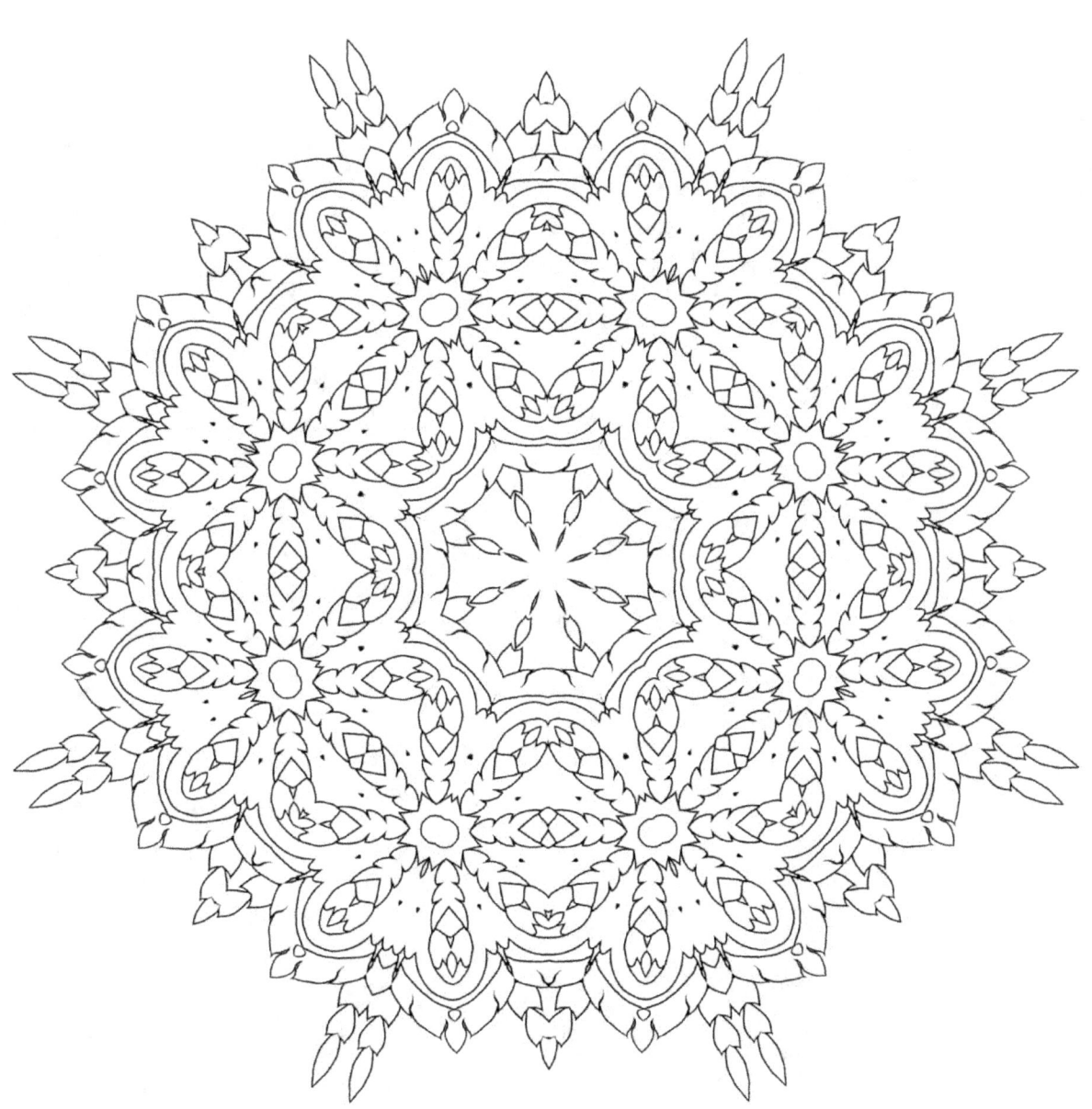

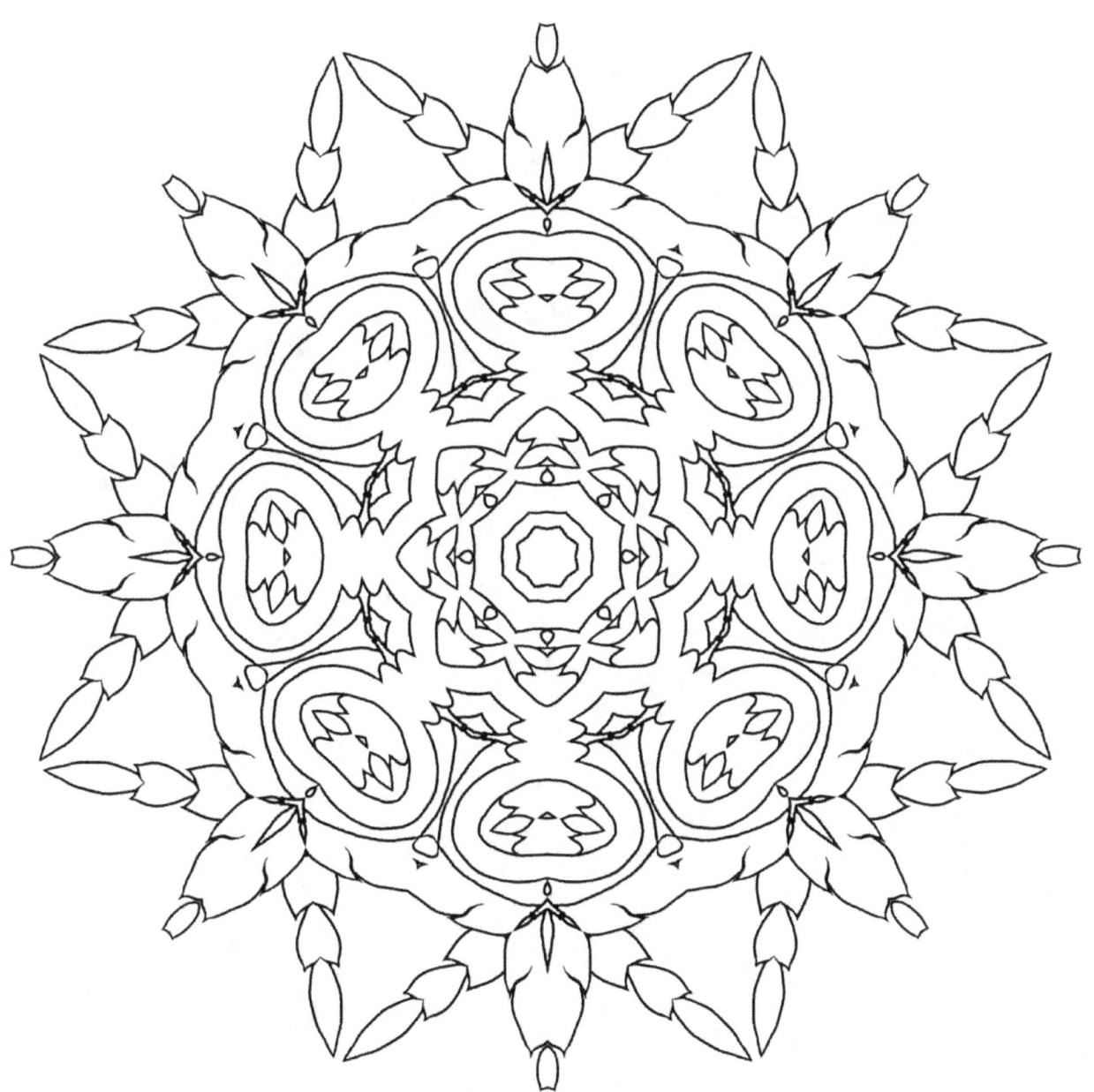

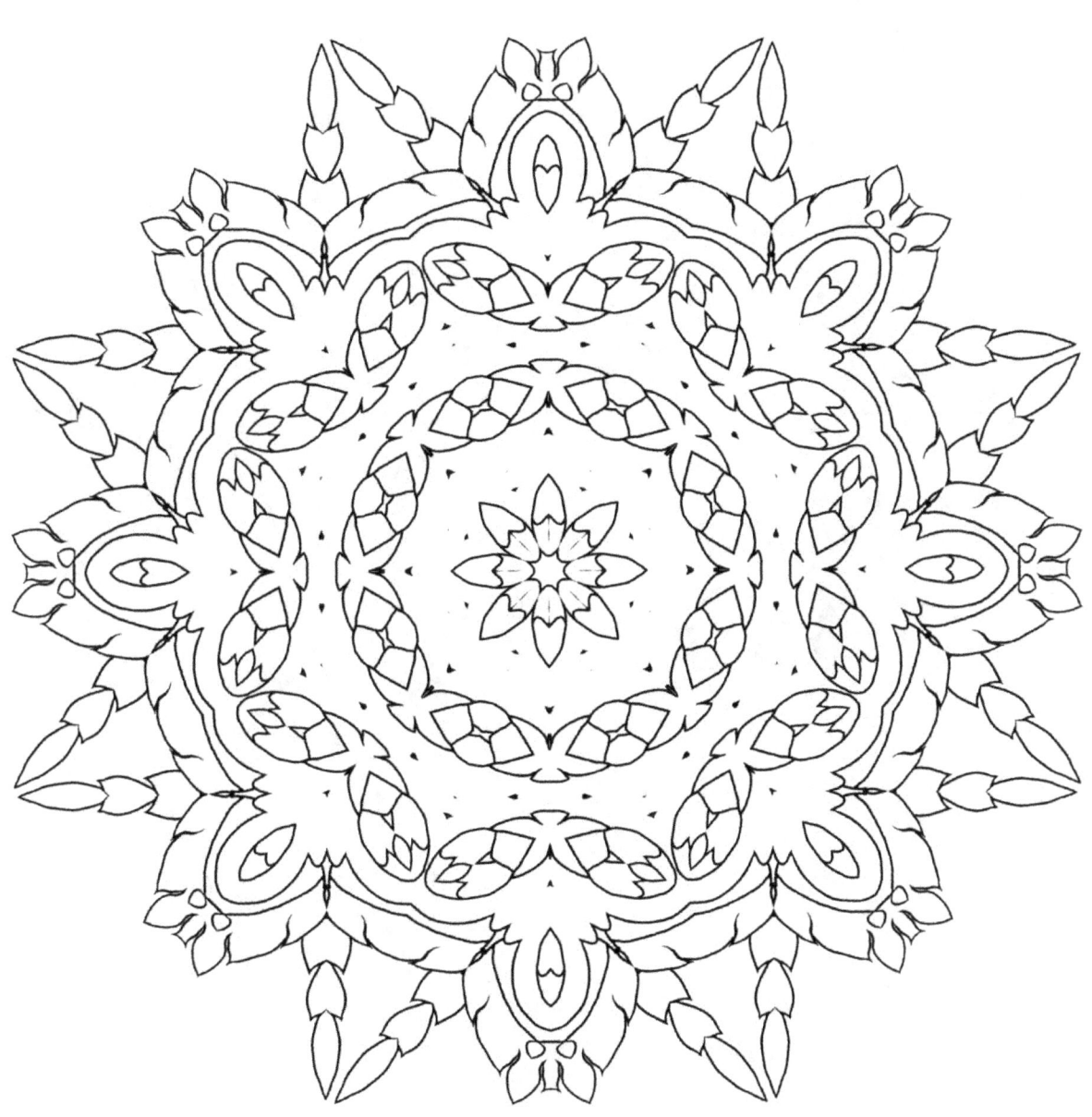

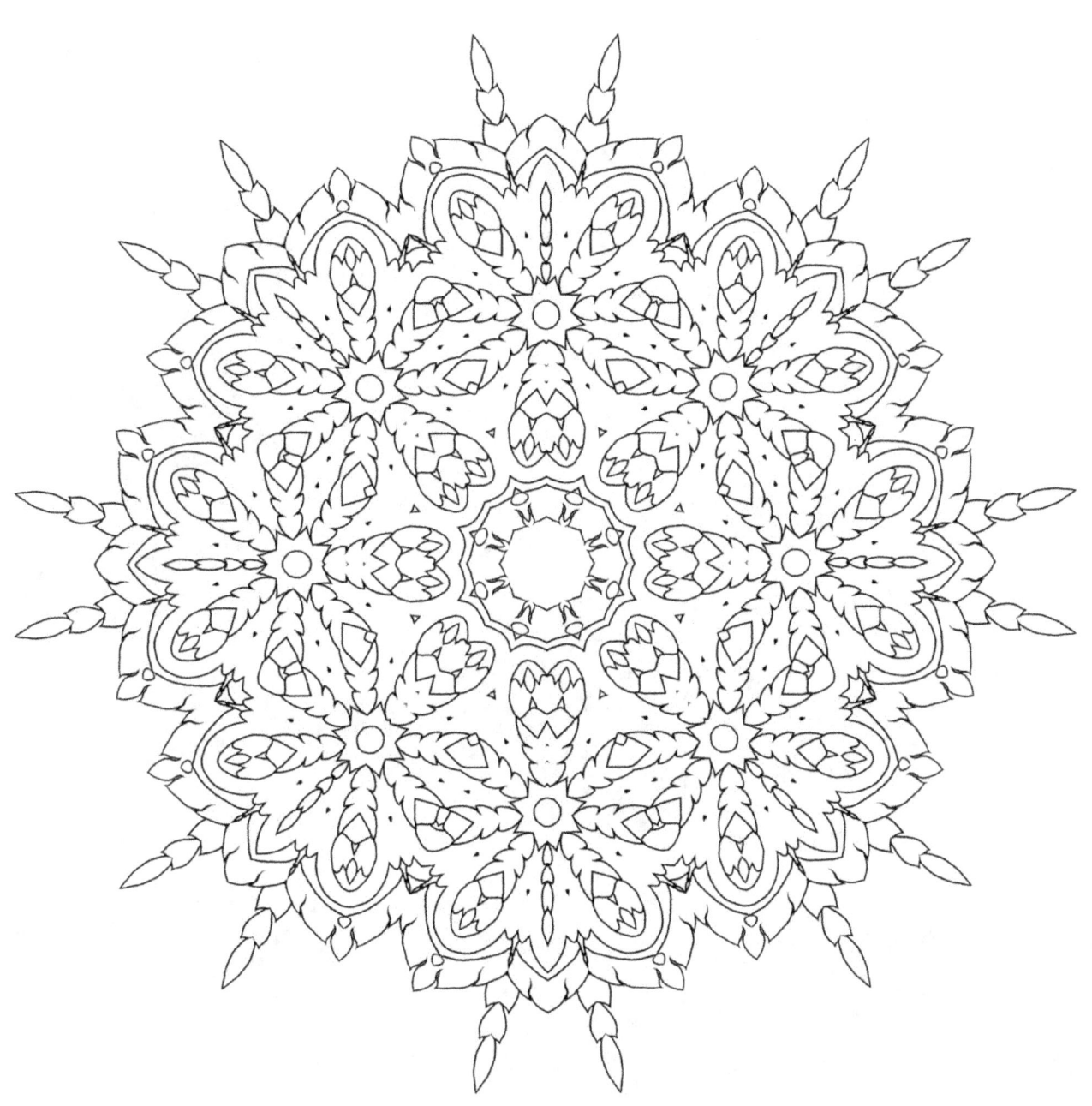

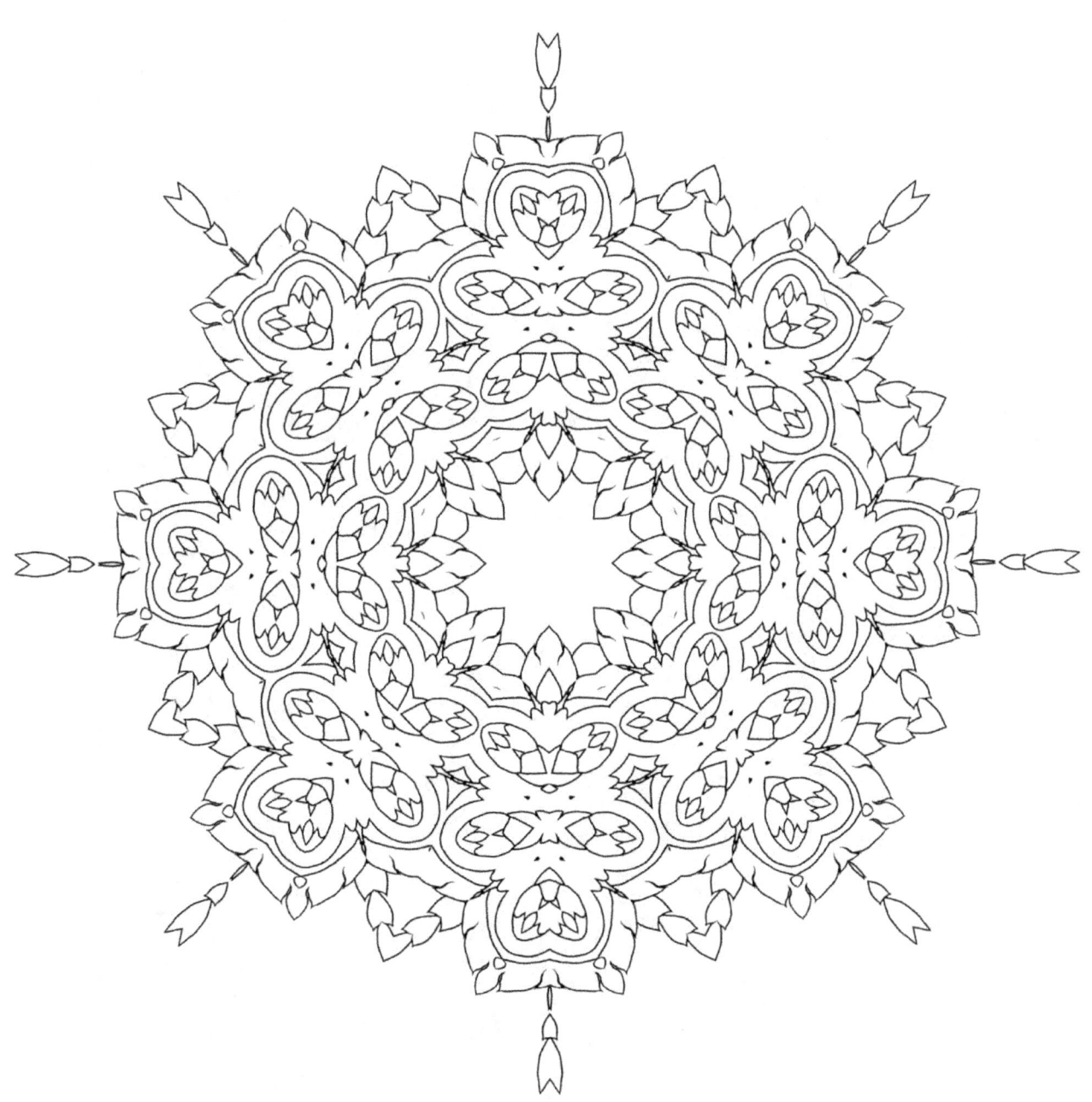

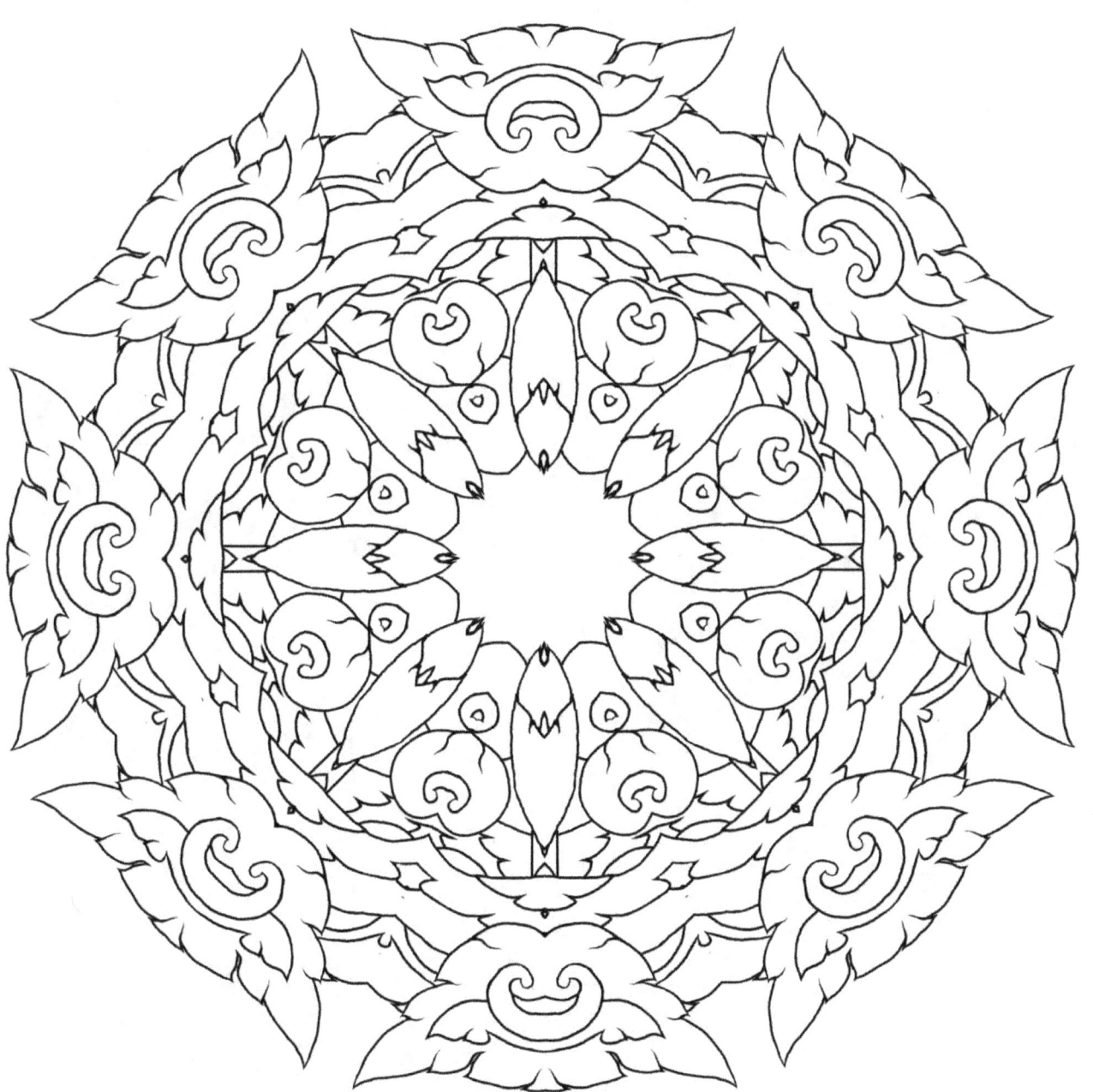

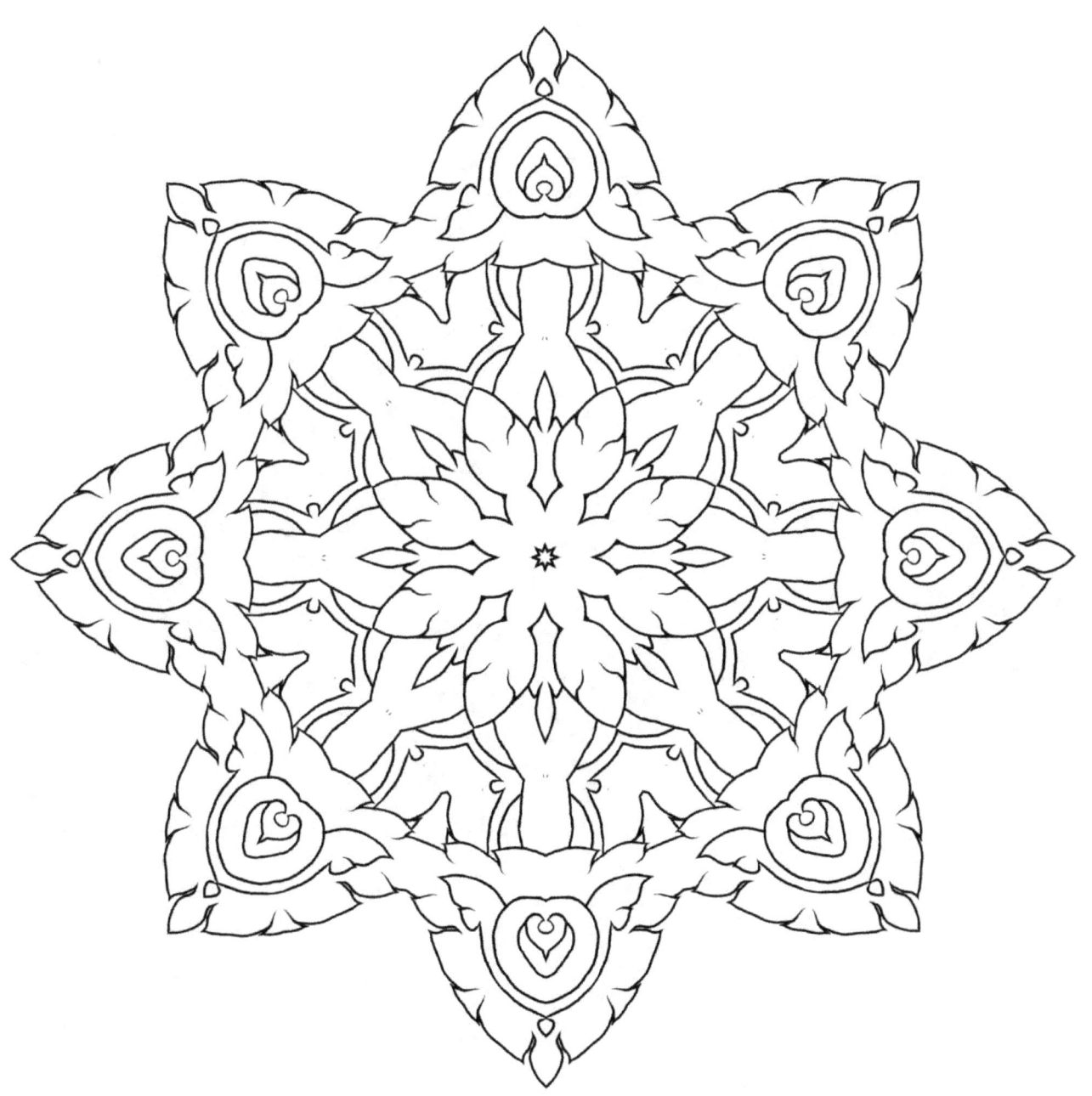

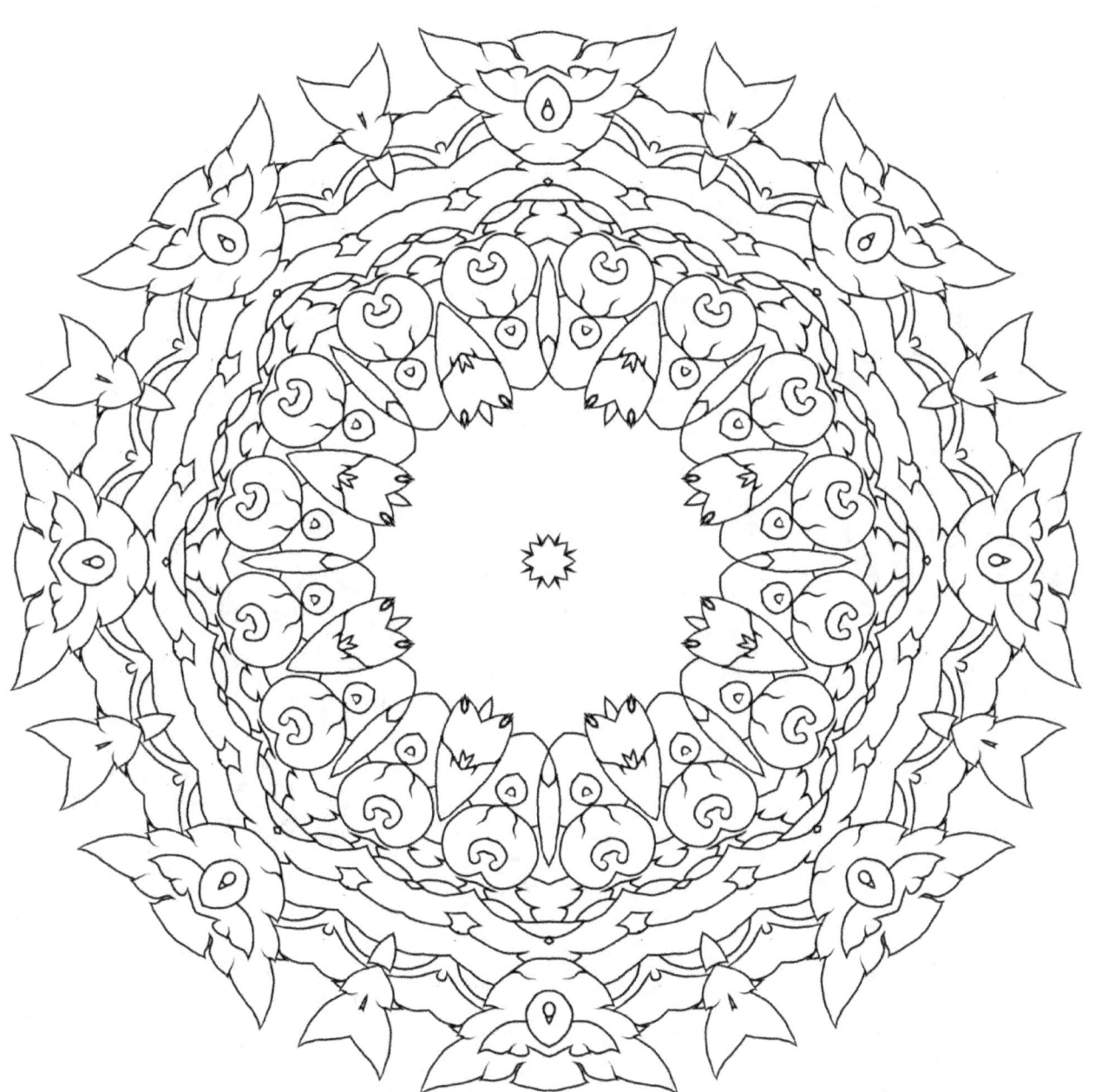

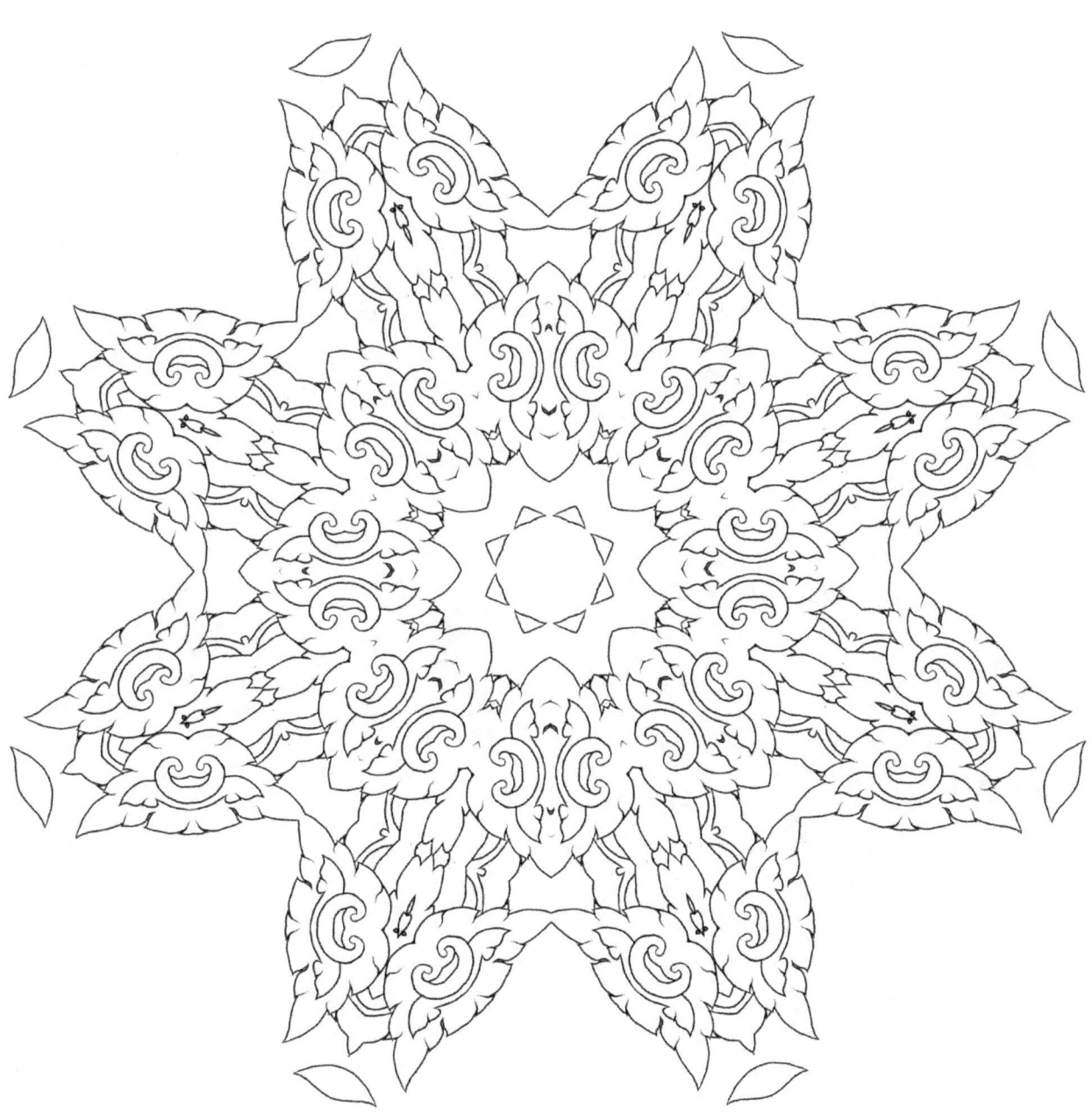

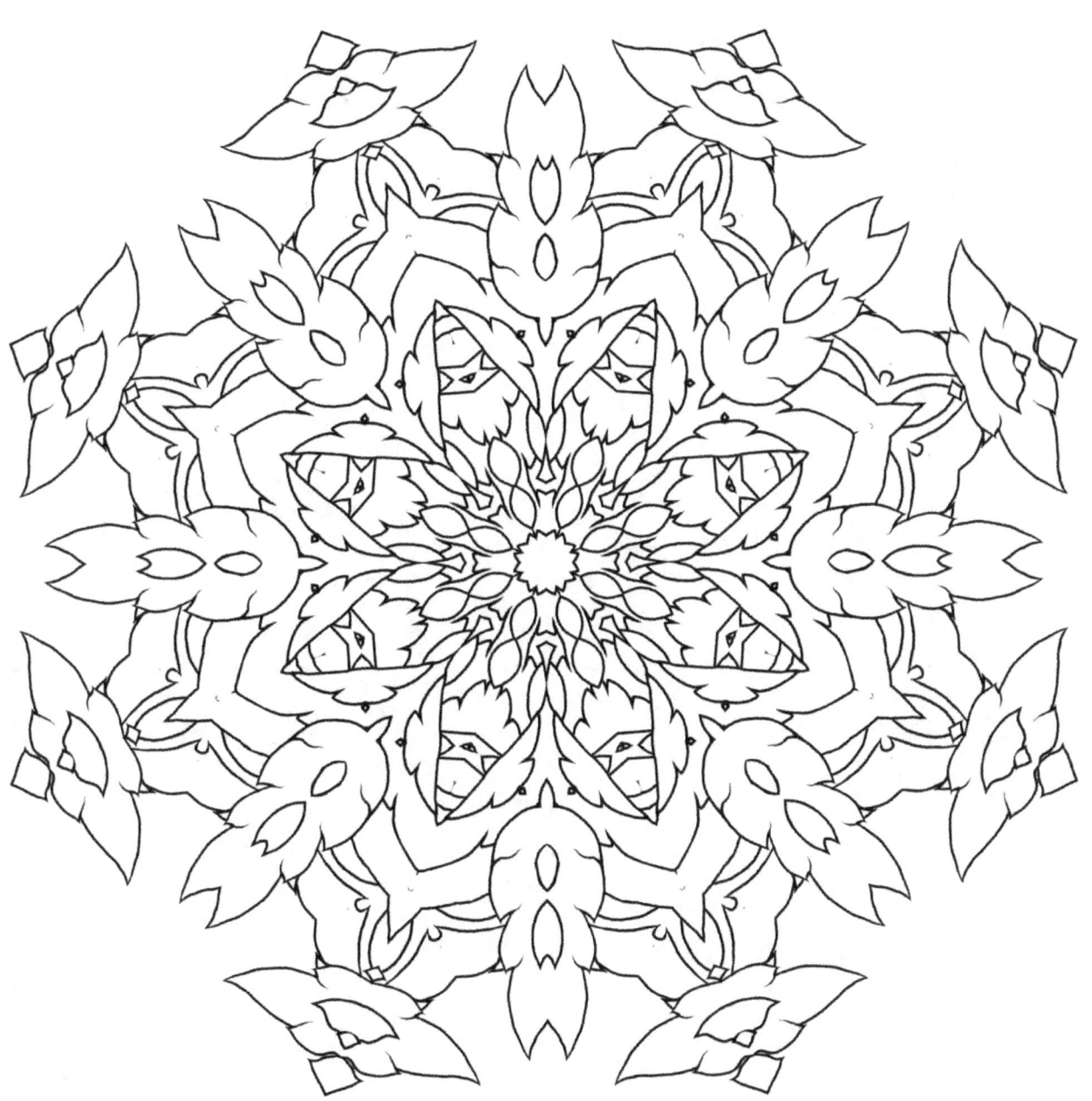

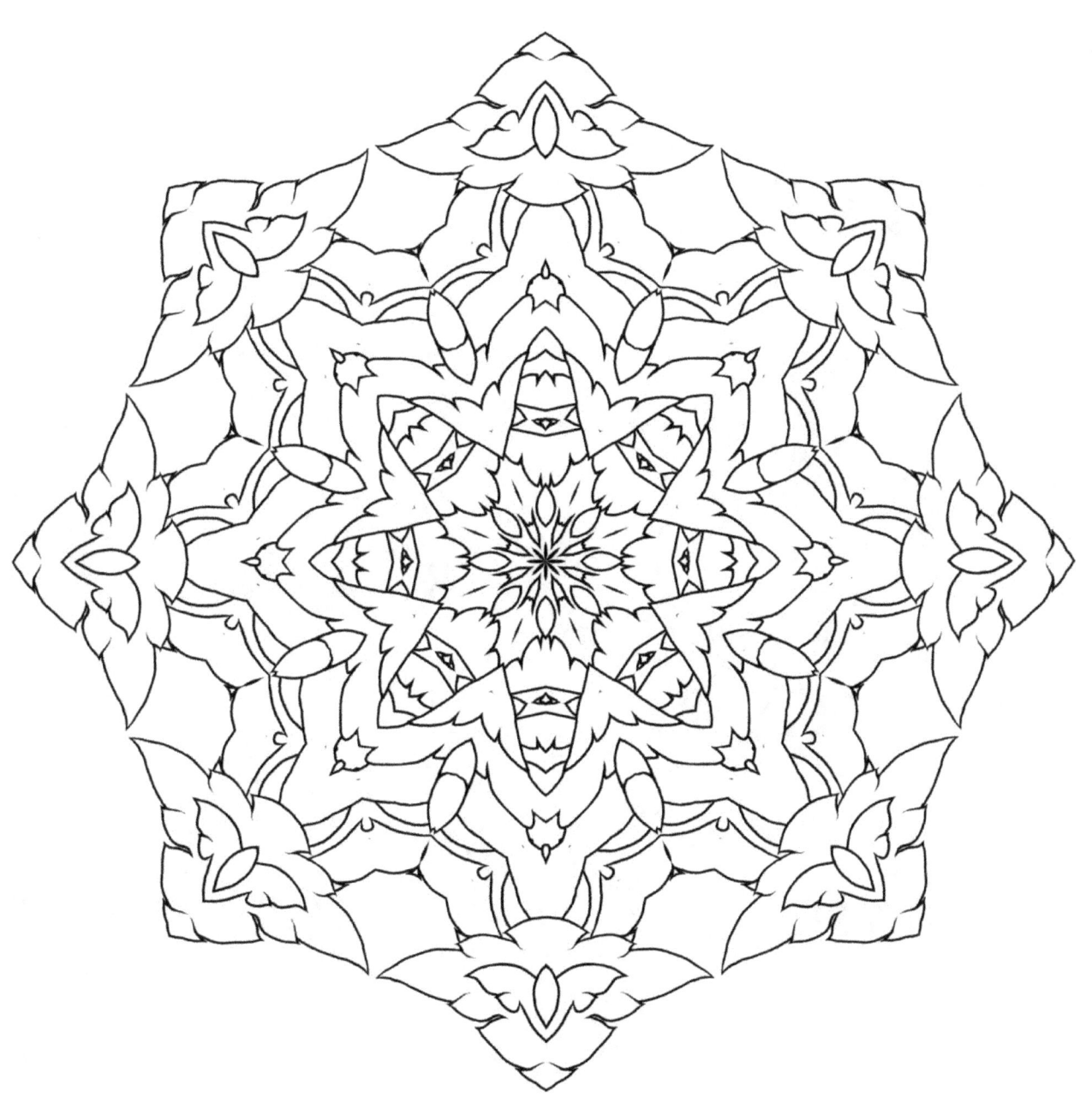

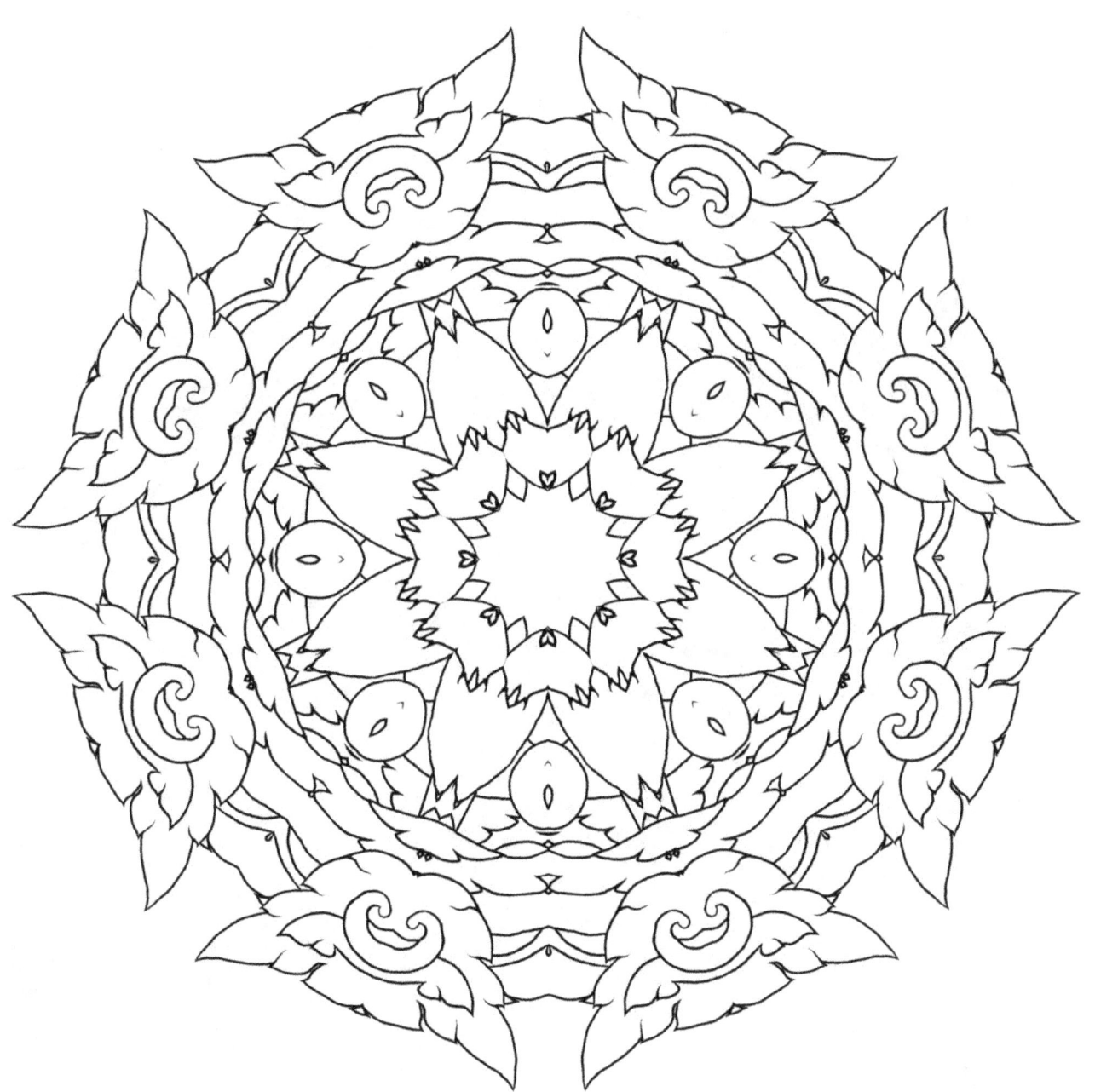

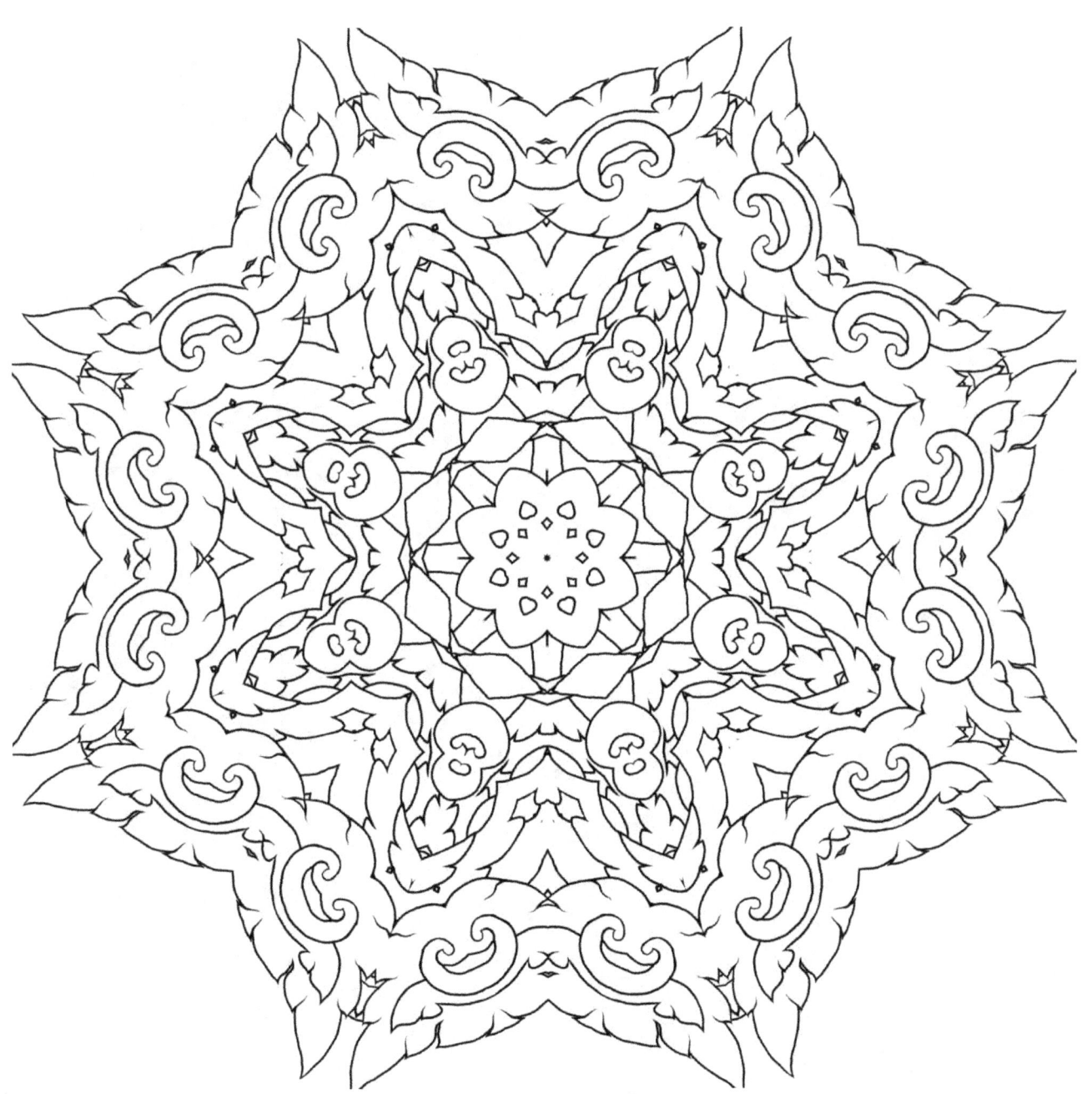

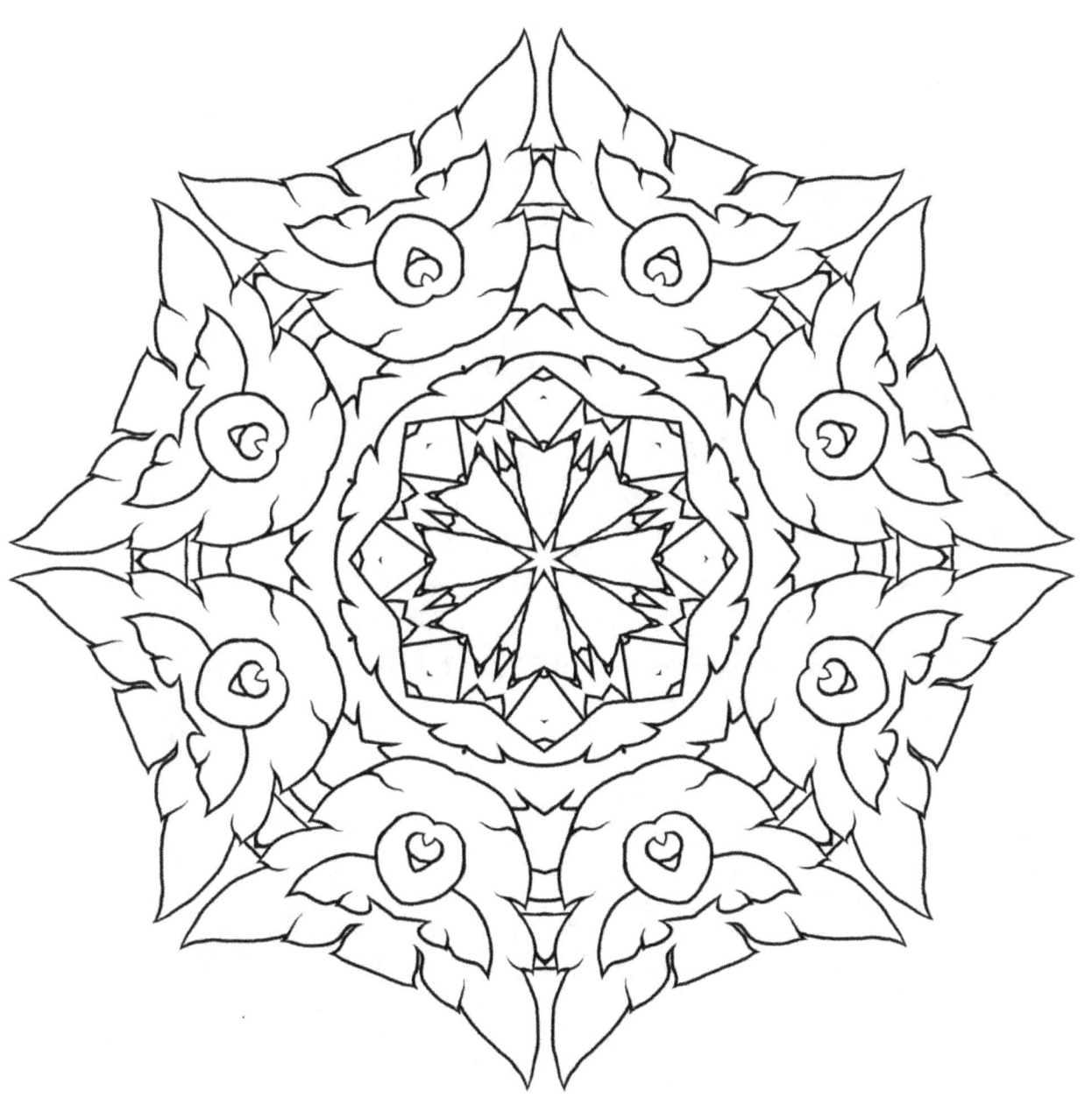

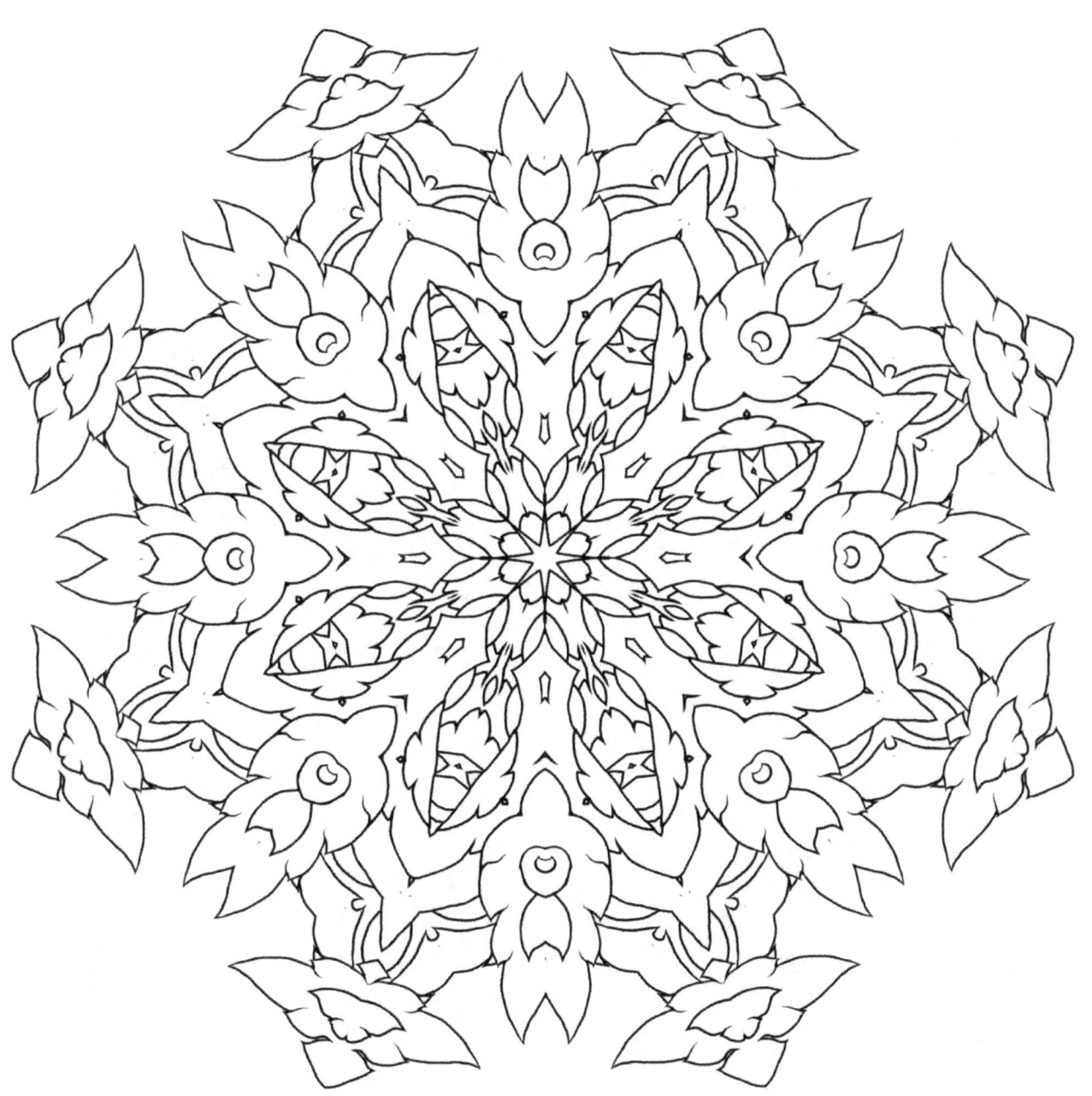

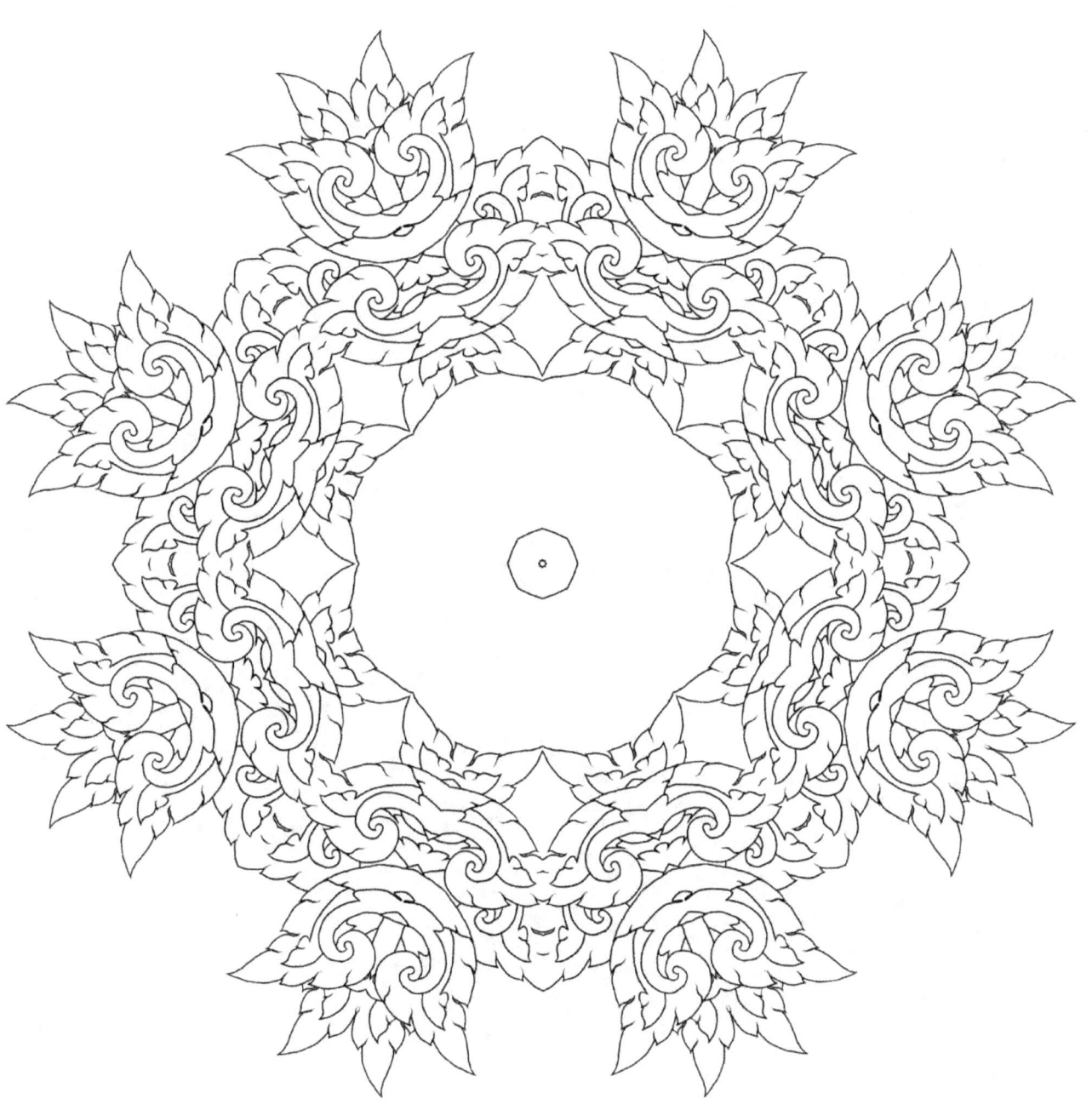

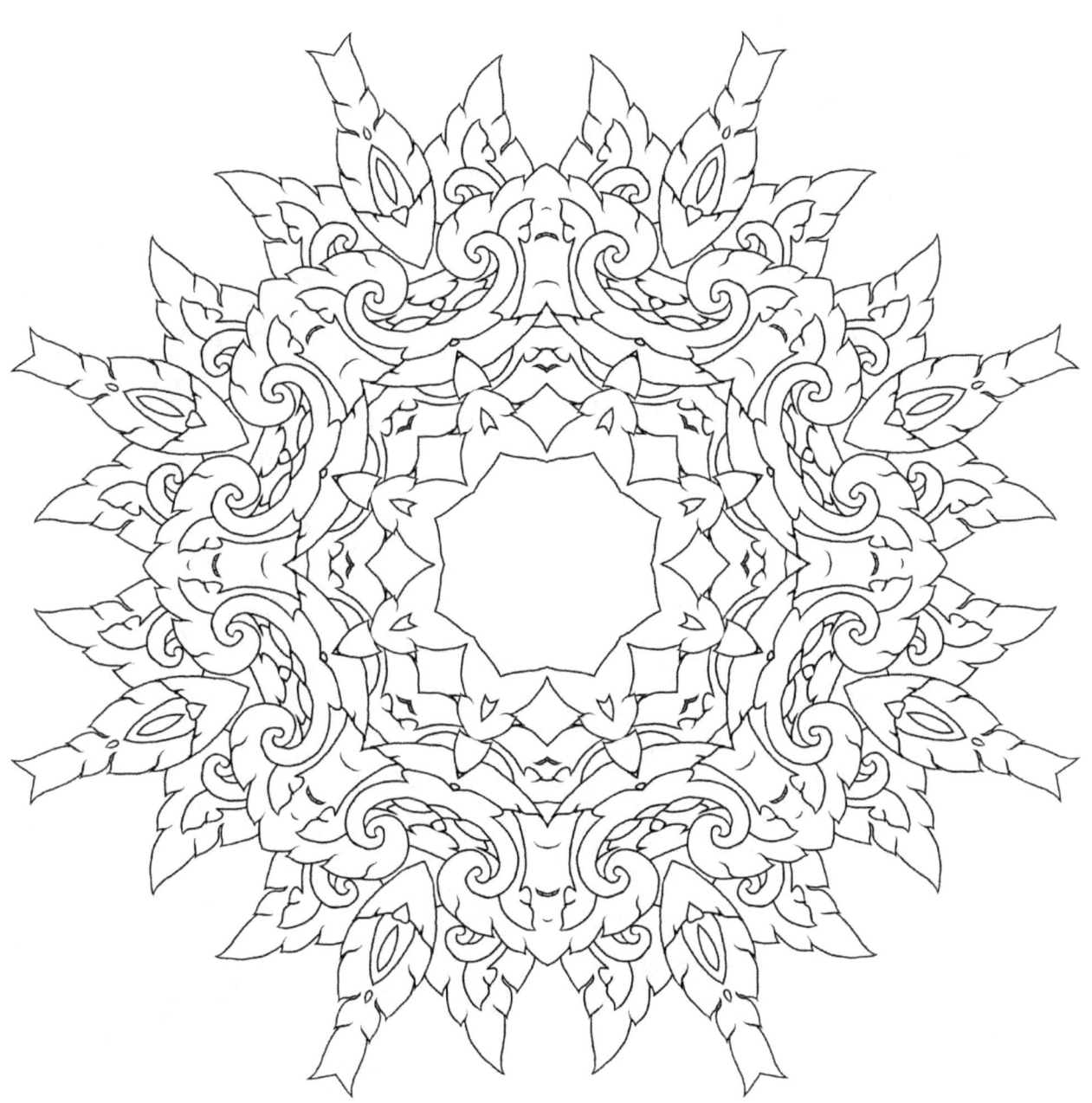

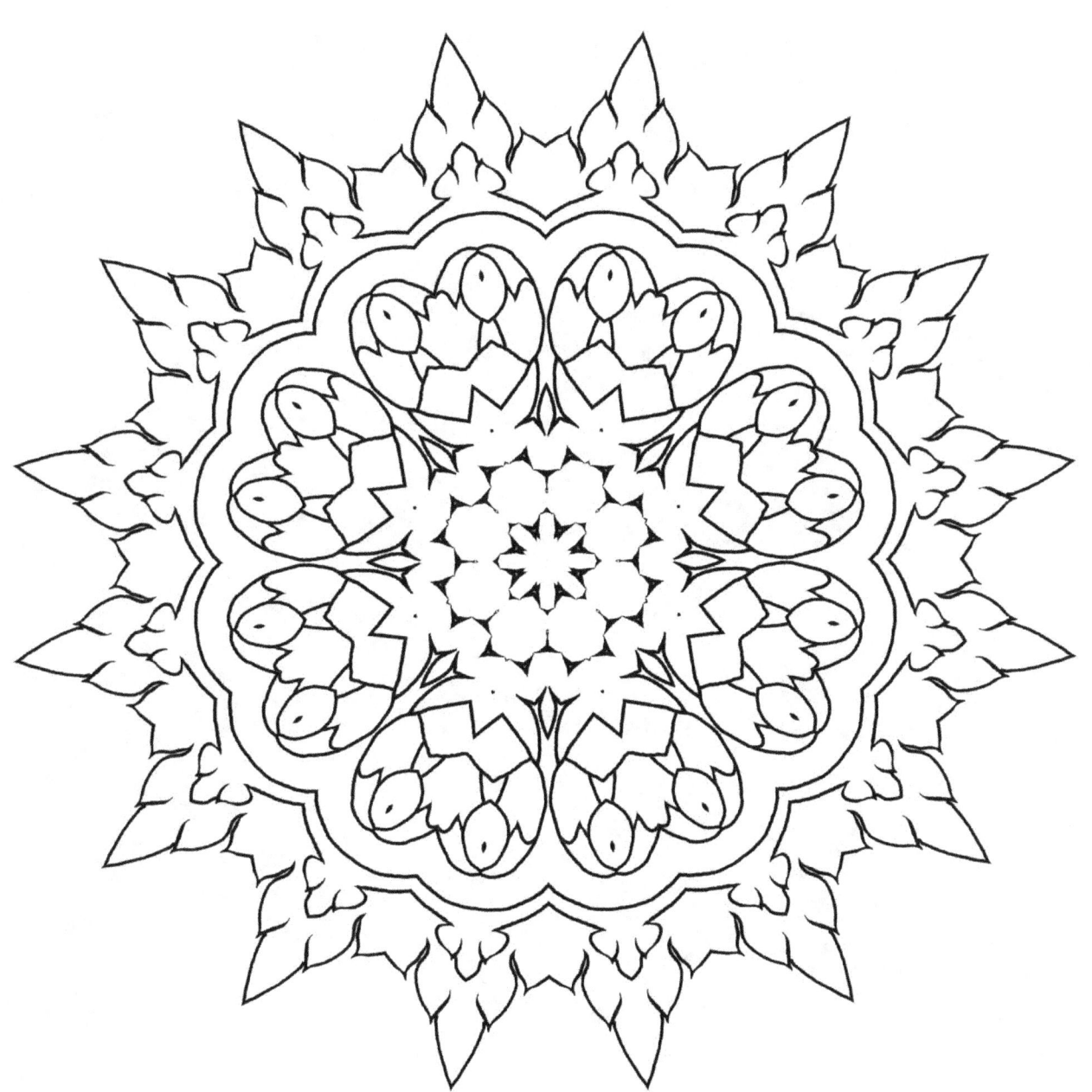

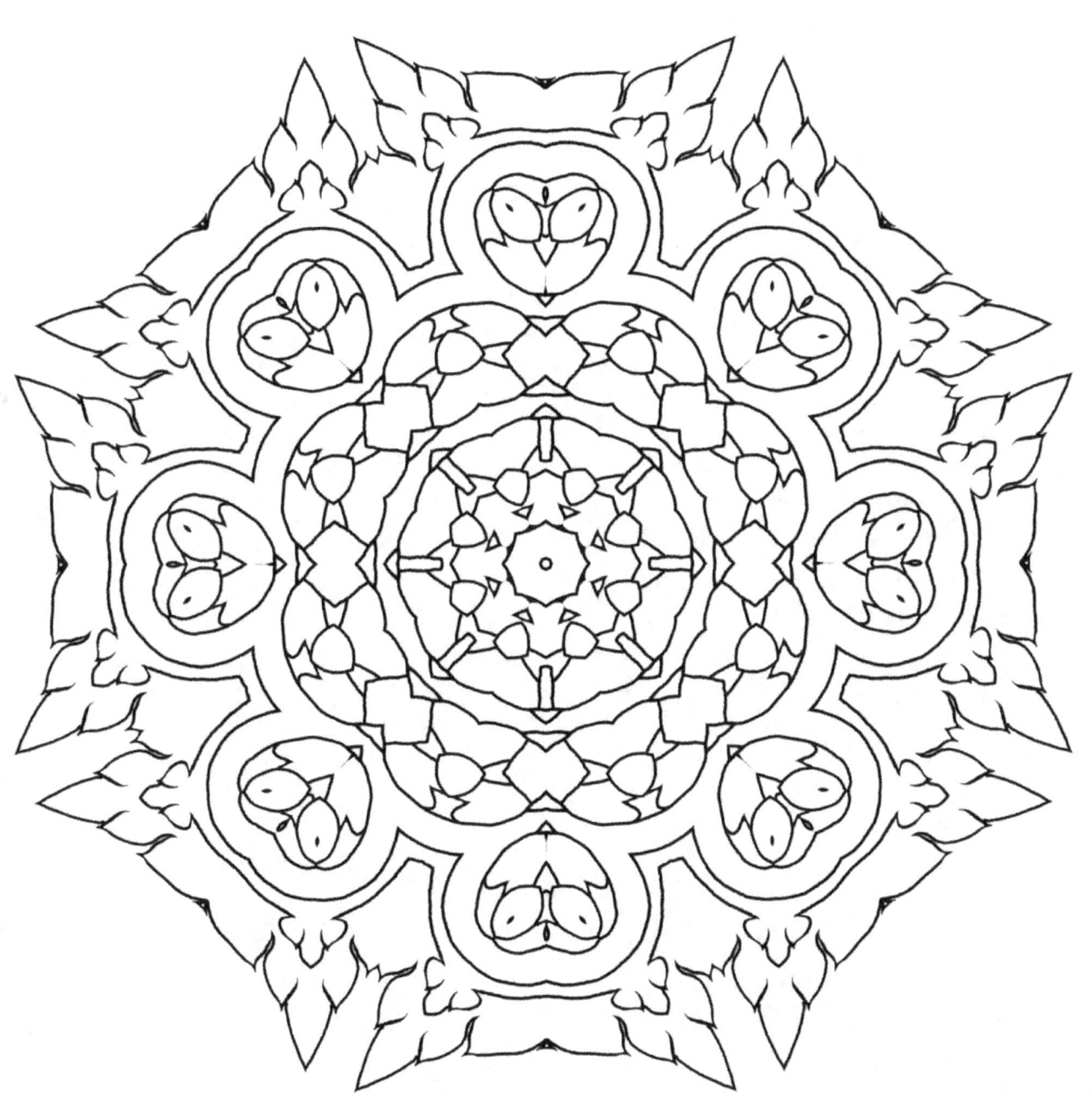

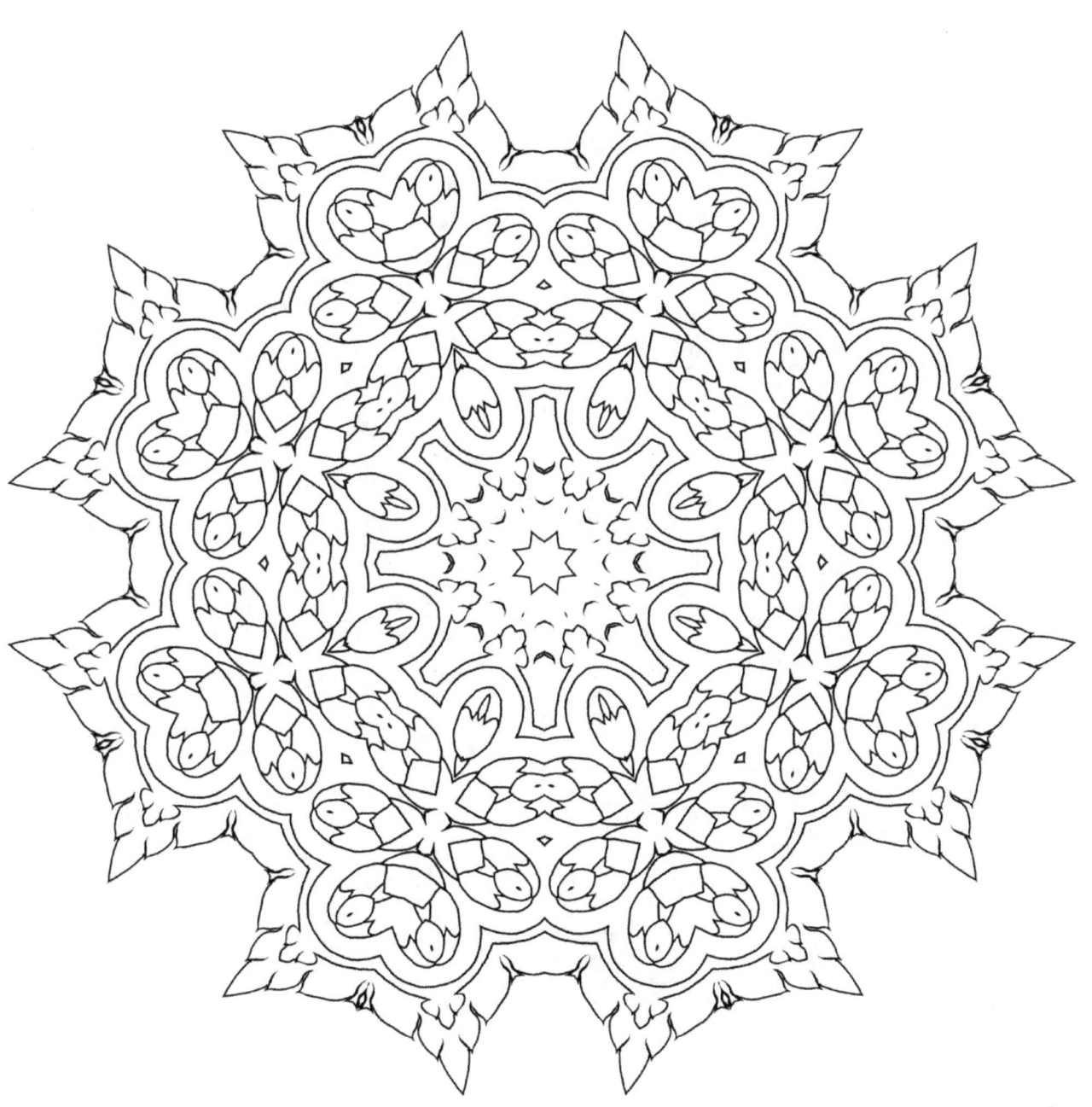

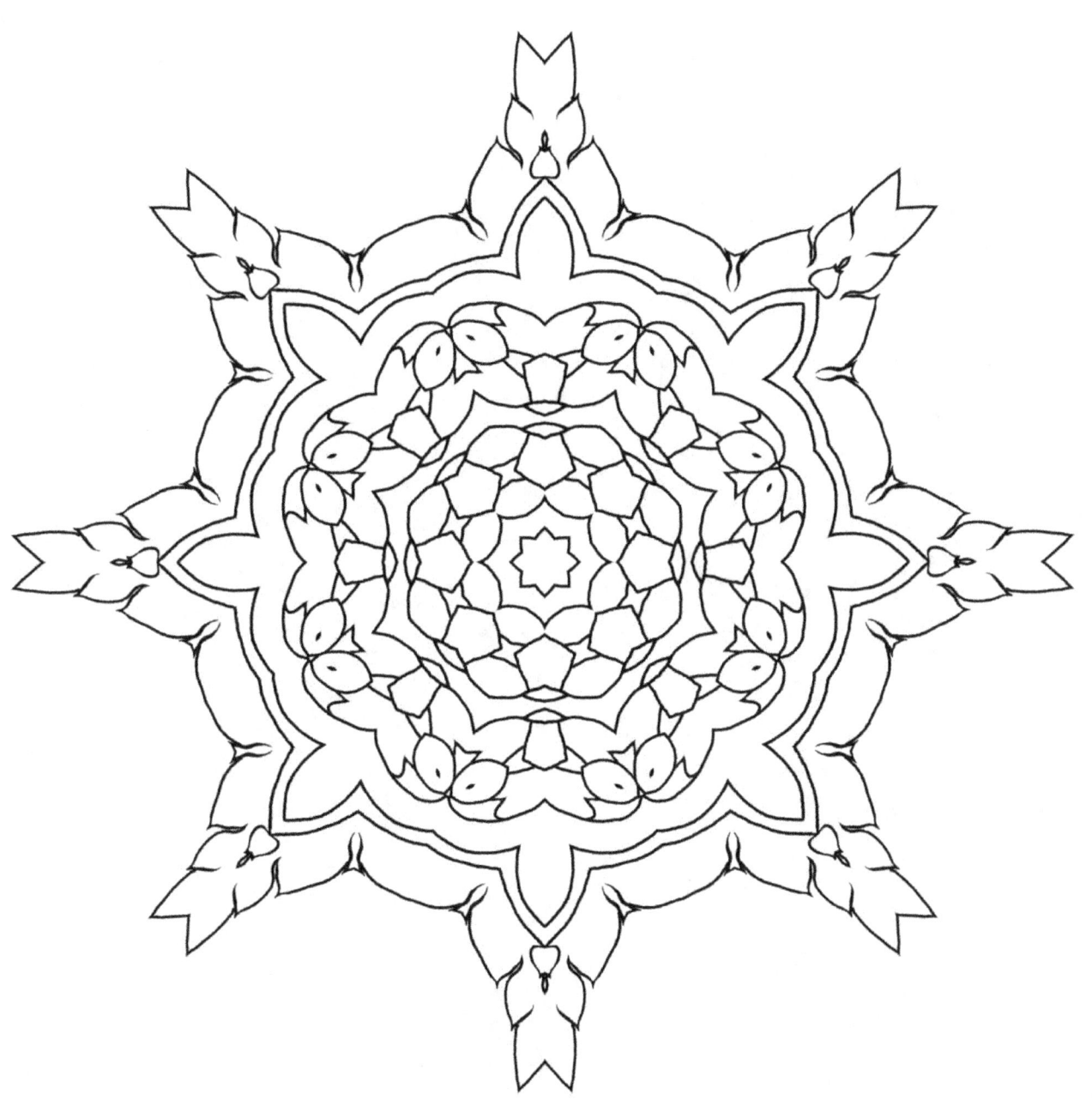

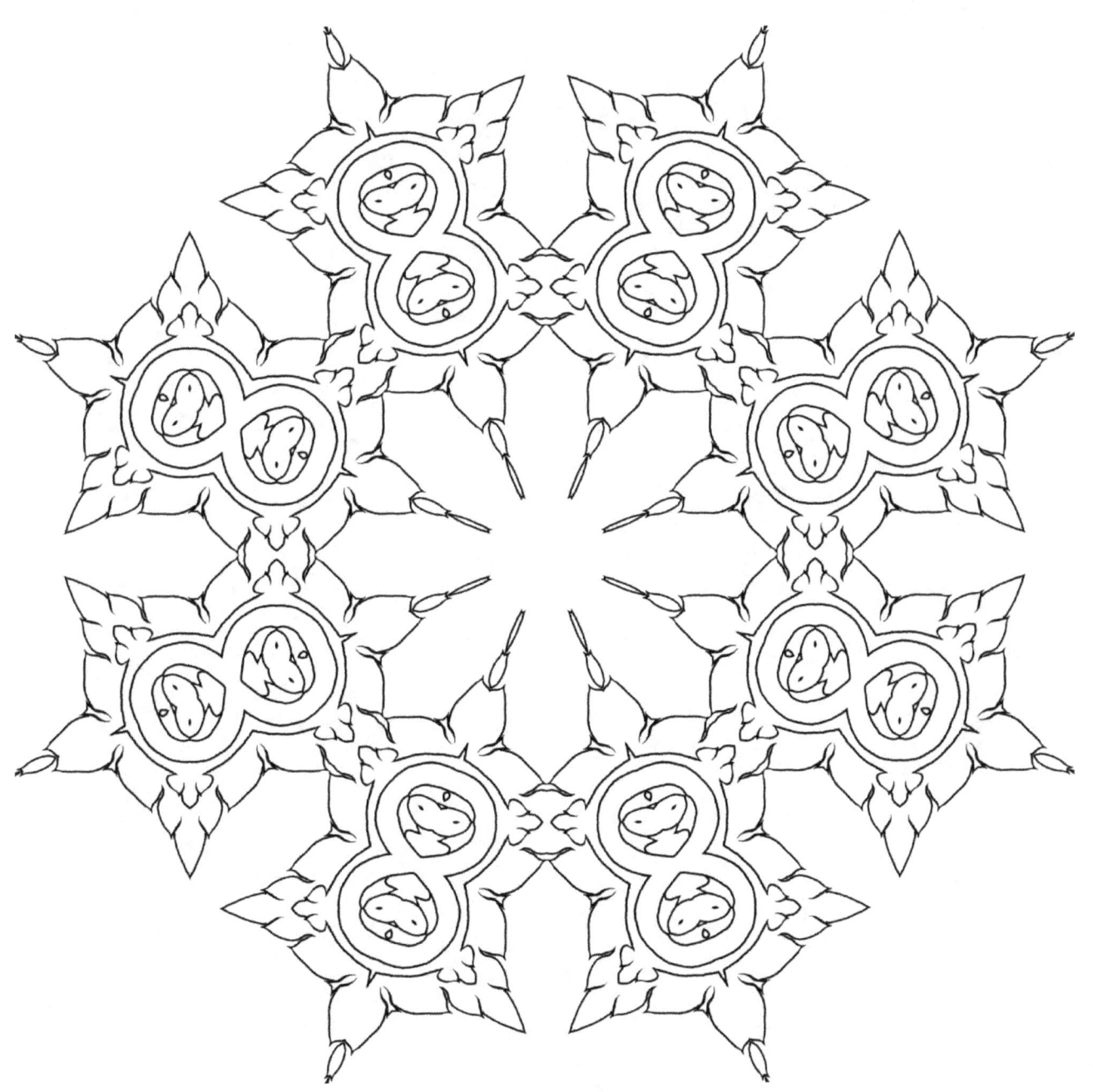

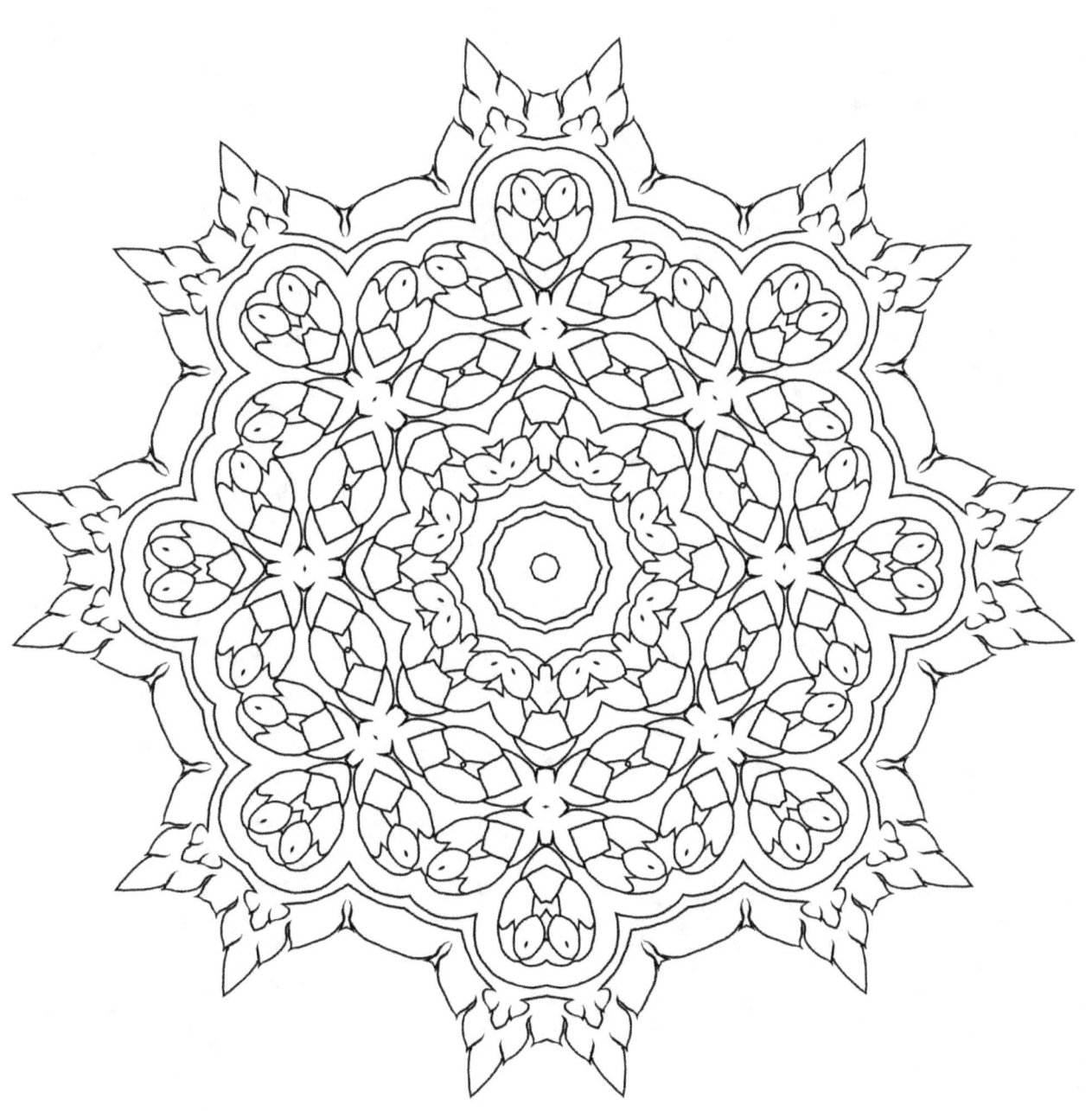

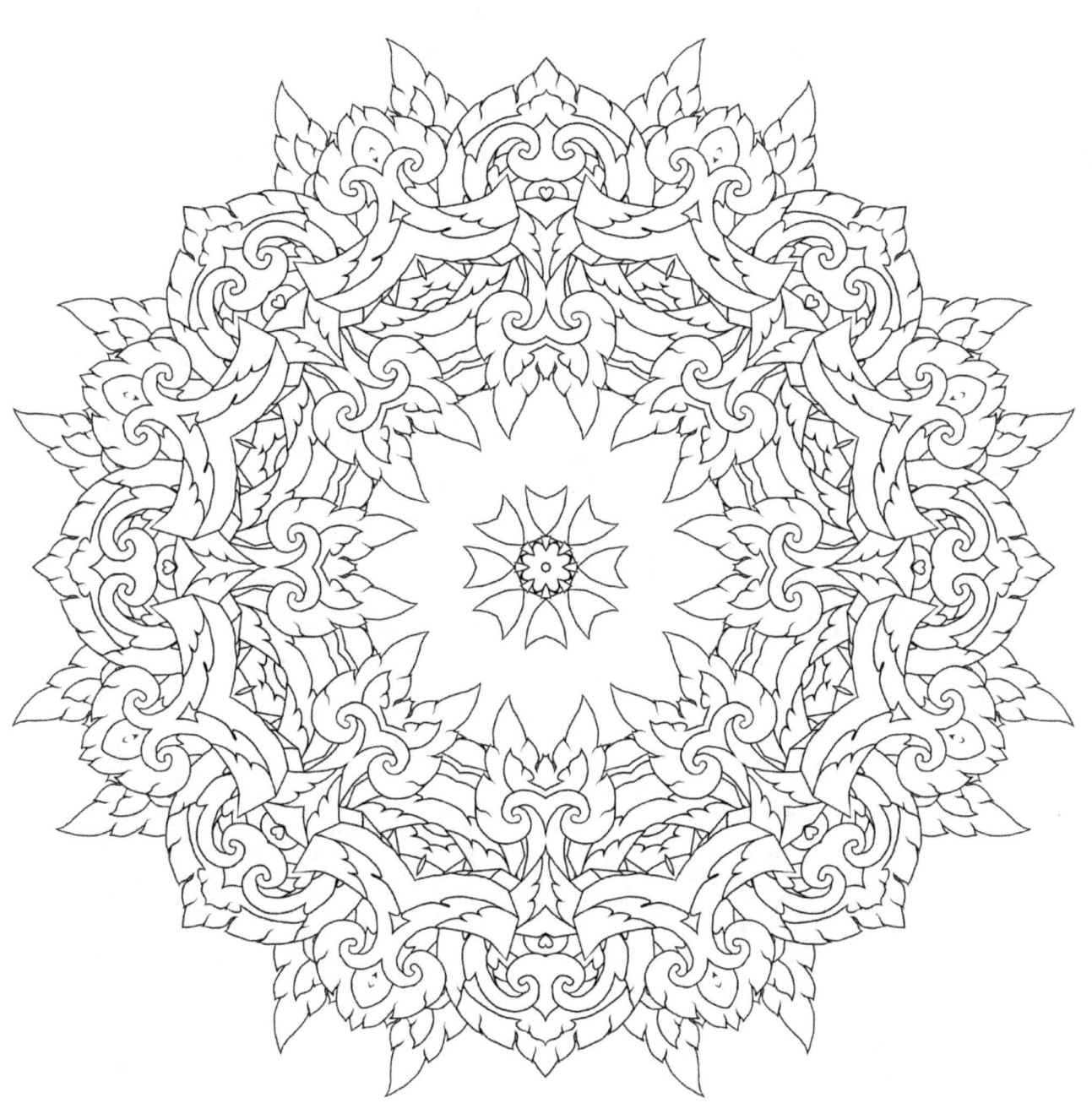

Thank you

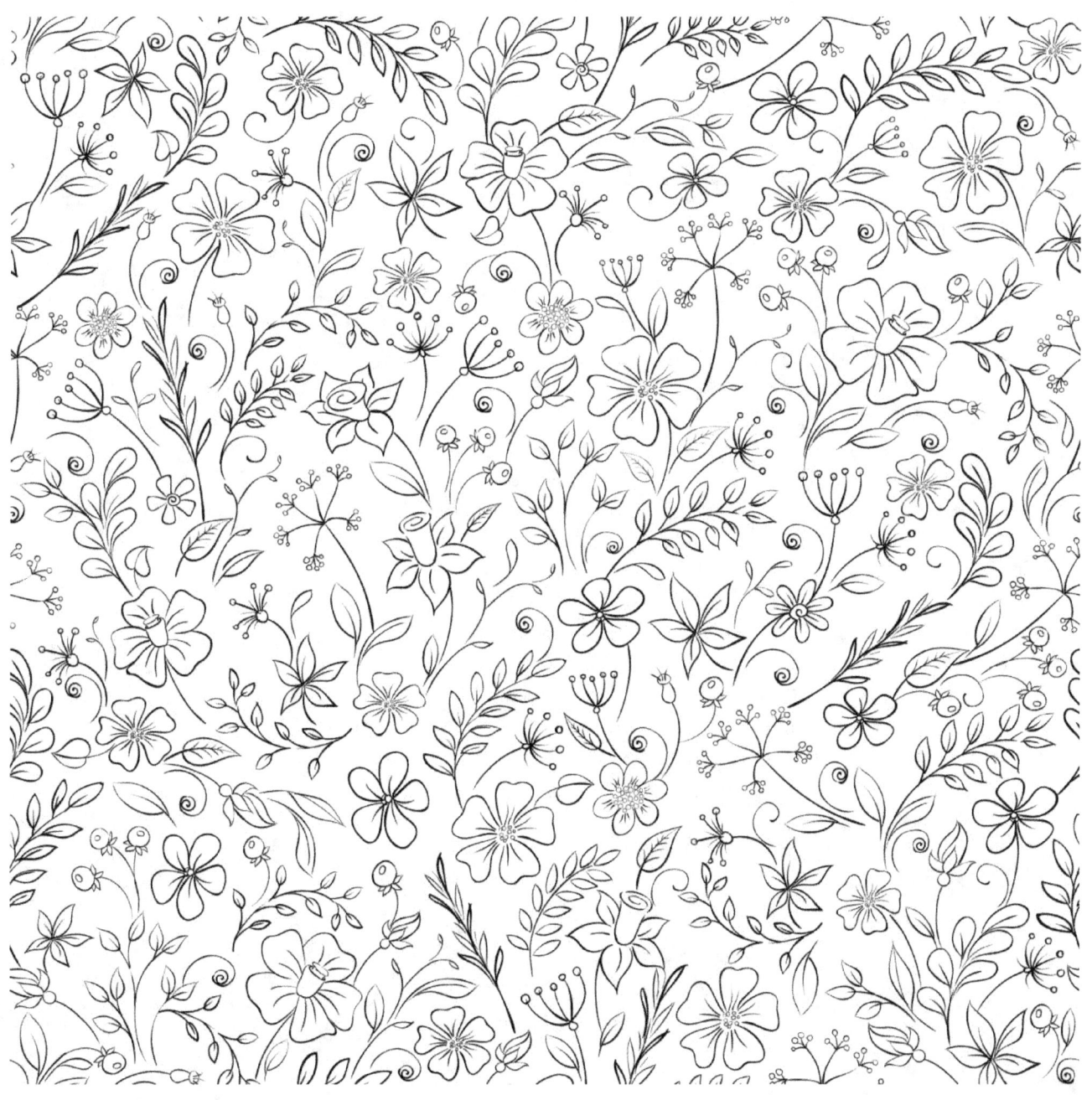

www.ingramcontent.com/pod-product-compliance
Lightning Source LLC
Chambersburg PA
CBHW081116180526
45170CB00008B/2875